HIGHER
MODERN STUDIES
REVISION GUIDE

 get **results**

Get Results Higher Modern Studies Revision Guide

Copyright © 2004 Imprint Publishing Systems Limited

ISBN 1 872 035 96 5

Printed in the United Kingdom by JSB Print, Glasgow.

Contents

Introduction

A consistent and structured approach to study over the whole length of your course is a major factor in achieving your potential in Higher Modern Studies. There is no substitute for regular study.

Revision, however, also has a very important role to play. Time becomes important – especially if you have several subjects to cover – and it is extremely unlikely that you will have sufficient time to read all your course notes over and over again. This revision guide provides a summarised version of the major Higher topics, presenting the most important materials in a structured way together with appropriate examples, facts and figures. You don't need to read it from cover to cover at one sitting – dip into it for as much or as little time as you have available.

WE hope that you will find the contents helpful.

Good Luck!

Politics in the United Kingdom
Decision Making in Central Government

WHAT THE SQA SAYS WILL BE IN THE EXAM

(a) Influences upon the decision-making process (pressures from groups, the media, public opinion); the extent of these pressures, their impact and legitimacy.

(b) Parliament as an arena for party conflict and decisions.

(c) The Executive (i.e. Prime Minister and the Cabinet); the power of the executive and its relationship with Parliament; relation to the machinery of government (e.g. government departments and agencies).

The Prime Minister

What are the powers of the Prime Minister?

♦ **The Prime Minister is the main spokesperson for the government**
When Tony Blair is interviewed on television, people listen carefully to what he has to say and any significant comment will be reported on other news programmes and in the newspapers.

♦ **The Prime Minister acts as a link between the Queen and Parliament**
Tony Blair will meet with the Queen on a weekly basis to keep her up to date with events in Parliament and government.

♦ **The Prime Minister appoints senior civil servants**
If civil servants want promotion, they will have to 'catch the eye' of the Prime Minister. This means that, where possible, they will try to get on his good side by finding evidence/writing reports to support the Prime Minister's views, e.g. when writing reports on the single currency they may direct their conclusions so that they support the views of the Prime Minister.

♦ **The Prime Minister appoints government ministers**
For example, Gordon Brown as Chancellor of the Exchequer and Jack Straw as Foreign Secretary. Members of Parliament who wish promotion will need to ensure that they are loyal to the Prime Minister and support party policy. Those who show ability may be promoted even if they do not always agree with the Prime Minister.

♦ **The Prime Minister reshuffles government ministers**
For example, Robin Cook was replaced by Jack Straw as Foreign Secretary after the 2001 general election.

♦ **The Prime Minister chairs Cabinet meetings and draws up the agenda**
This allows the Prime Minister to decide which issues should be discussed and in what order. Issues he considers

Tony Blair

to be important will be discussed at the start of the meeting, leaving less important or indeed more difficult issues to the end of the meeting, when there is less time available. Under Tony Blair, the Cabinet only meets for 1 hour a week. Most of the work takes place in the Cabinet's 50 committees and sub-committees. There is not enough time for the Prime Minister and Cabinet Ministers to be directly involved in all meetings, therefore Ministers tend to focus on their departments and the Prime Minister will concentrate on one or two key issues, e.g. the war in Iraq, 'foundation hospitals' or 'university top-up fees'.

♦ **The Prime Minister is responsible for the production of Cabinet minutes**
The Prime Minister keeps notes of discussions and decisions made in Cabinet and decides on the information to be included, e.g. when Robin Cook and Clare Short resigned from the government, Tony Blair may have only noted positive comments about them and left out any negative views.

◆ **The Prime Minister derives power from within his own party**

The Prime Minister is likely to receive the backing of ambitious party members on controversial issues such as public/private partnerships. To ensure the support of his party, he tries to attend most of the meetings of the Parliamentary Labour Party which take place just before 'Prime Minister's Questions' on a Wednesday.

◆ **The Prime Minister controls the timetable of the government**

Parliament cannot deal with all the issues at once. When Tony Blair came to power in 1997, he decided that it was more important to establish the Scottish Parliament and leave other constitutional reforms such as the reform of the House of Lords and electoral system until later.

◆ **The Prime Minister controls the Honours System**

People who want to be on the Honours List are likely to support the person who can put them there. John Major, the last Conservative prime minister, appointed 171 life peers in the 7 years he was in office. Tony Blair appointed 150 in his first 5 years. This power may change with the proposed reforms to the House of Lords. The Appointments Commission now selects crossbench members of the House of Lords.

◆ **The Prime Minister represents the country internationally**

The Prime Minister receives positive publicity from attending meetings with other world leaders. European Union Summits, for example, attract substantial news coverage.

◆ **The Prime Minister decides the timing of the general election**

A general election must be held at most every 5 years. However, it is common for the Prime Minister to call an election before the end of the 5 year period. Tony Blair was first elected in 1997 and decided to go to the polls in May 2001 because he knew that he had an excellent chance to secure a second term in office.

◆ **The Prime Minister is affected by the size of his party's majority**

Tony Blair secured a large majority in Parliament in 1997 and again in 2001. This means that it is much easier to ensure that new legislation is approved by Parliament. Tony Blair actually spends little time in Parliament. He has only voted in about 3% of votes and usually only attends for 'Prime Minister's Questions'. The present majority of 167 is very different from the end of John Major's term in office when he had no majority, thus making it very difficult for legislation to be passed by Parliament.

◆ **The Prime Minister benefits from the Whip system**

The Whip system is used to ensure that enough MPs vote with their party. If they do not support their party, then all parliamentary privileges may be withdrawn.

◆ **The Prime Minister has special foreign and defence responsibilities**

Parliament can debate issues such as military action in Afghanistan or Iraq but the decision to use armed forces rests with the Prime Minister.

What are the limitations on the powers of the Prime Minister?

◆ **An election every five years**

In 1997, John Major did not want to call a general election as he realised that it was going to be very difficult for the Conservative Party to be re-elected. However, there was no choice as Parliament's five year term had expired. In the election, the Conservatives lost a large number of seats, giving Labour victory with an overall majority of 179.

◆ **The Whip system**

The Whip system is a two-way process. If MPs are unhappy with the way the government is handling a particular issue, they can pass on their concerns to the Whips or even vote against the government. In 2001, the Labour Government was defeated on its nominations to Select Committees because many MPs thought that the Prime Minister did not like the outgoing Chairs of the Transport and Foreign Affairs Committees (Gwyneth Dunwoody and Donald Anderson) as they had been critical of the government.

◆ **Prime Minister's Questions**

Every Wednesday, the Prime Minister must answer questions in the House of Commons for 30 minutes. If he does not perform well, particularly in response to the Conservative leader, then it may result in damage to his reputation and a possible loss of support. Many would argue that William Hague came out well in his exchanges with Tony Blair, while Iain Duncan Smith did less well. First indications are that Michael Howard, the new Leader of the Opposition, will be a strong performer at Prime Minister's Questions.

Michael Howard

Balance of opinion

When appointing members of the Cabinet, the Prime Minister will often try to ensure a balance of party opinion. This may mean that he does not always get his own way in Cabinet. The Prime Minister is sometimes described as 'first among equals' and this means that, if the majority of the Cabinet was against the Prime Minister, it would not be advisable to ignore their opinions.

The size of the government majority

Towards the end of his premiership, John Major did not have a majority in the House of Commons. This made life very difficult for him and much time and effort had to be devoted to managing the voting of his own party's MPs.

The House of Lords can delay bills (not money bills) for up to one year

This means that important legislation may be delayed, making it more difficult for the government to carry out manifesto commitments. For example, the House of Lords voted against the government's proposals for the privatisation of Air Traffic Control.

The mass media

If the media turns against the Prime Minister then it may encourage people to vote against him. The Prime Minister must be 'on the ball' 24 hours a day, 7 days a week as any small mistake may be used against him. Tony Blair puts strong emphasis on media relations and doubled the number of special advisers from 40 to 80. Tony Blair is worried that, if he supports the Single European Currency, the press will turn against him and he will find it difficult to win the next election. The media can also use information to damage the government. In 2002, a row between Stephen Byers and his chief information officer, Martin Sixsmith, damaged the government's credibility. Peter Mandelson was forced to resign when the press revealed that he was involved in trying to obtain passports for the Hinduja brothers. Robin Cook and Clare Short resigned over the war in Iraq.

Events

The Prime Minister has to manage any unexpected events. Fuel protests, Foot and Mouth, 9/11 and the death of Doctor David Kelly are good examples of how events can quickly bring the Prime Minister's handling of a situation under scrutiny. Sometimes a member of the Cabinet disagrees and this can make the government seem weak and divided.

Party chooses the leader

All Prime Ministers since 1945 have been the leaders of their parties. This also means that the leader can be challenged. In 1990, Michael Heseltine challenged Margaret Thatcher for the leadership of the Conservative Party. Eventually she was ousted and John Major became the new party leader.

Parliamentary committees

Select Committees can call the Prime Minister to give evidence and can scrutinise the work of government departments.

The Cabinet

The Cabinet has about 25 members and consists of the Prime Minister and his senior government colleagues including the Chancellor of the Exchequer, the Foreign Secretary and the Home Secretary.

Cabinet Table Layout

1. Prime Minister
2. Deputy Prime Minister
3. Cabinet Secretary
4. Chancellor of the Exchequer
5. Home Secretary
6. Foreign Secretary
7. Junior Cabinet Ministers
8. Middle Ranking Cabinet Ministers

What are the powers of the Cabinet?

The Cabinet will make, check or endorse major government decisions

For example, the Cabinet considered how to respond to the events of 9/11 in the USA in 2001.

The Cabinet settles disputes between government departments

For example, the Chancellor of the Exchequer may want to cut back on defence spending and put more resources into health and education. Rather than falling out in public, ministers can discuss the issues in Cabinet and hopefully come to a compromise.

The Cabinet will discuss issues and agree on government policy

When a decision has been reached, all members of the Cabinet must support that decision. This is called 'collective responsibility'. For example, if individual members of the Cabinet disagree about proposals for university top-up fees, once a decision is made they must support it in public. Their only alternative is to resign as Robin Cook and Clare Short did over the war in Iraq.

◆ **The Cabinet will evaluate the success or failure of government initiatives**

If it is felt that a government department is not working effectively, then the Cabinet may make suggestions that will result in improvement. Thus, during the Foot and Mouth crisis in 2001, it may have considered that the outbreak was not being dealt with properly and suggested that it was sufficiently important for the Prime Minister to take charge.

◆ **The Cabinet meets every week**

This will provide ministers with access to the Prime Minister, giving them the opportunity to impress or to persuade the Prime Minister to change his opinion on certain issues.

What are the limitations on the powers of the Cabinet?

◆ **Collective responsibility**

As the Cabinet is bound by the doctrine of 'collective responsibility', members have to support all government policies in public. This may be difficult when they do not agree with the policies. Sometimes individuals feel so strongly that they have to resign from the Cabinet.

◆ **The Prime Minister is responsible for selecting Cabinet ministers**

In the past, the Prime Minister would try to ensure that there was a cross-section of party opinion within the Cabinet. However, this is no longer the case. Many would argue that Tony Blair has appointed his own supporters to the Cabinet. This may mean that the Cabinet becomes a 'rubber stamp' for the decisions of the Prime Minister.

◆ **The Cabinet does not always have time to discuss the detail behind decisions**

The Cabinet therefore has to make decisions without always having detailed information. It may also mean that Cabinet Committees have to deal with certain issues.

◆ **If Cabinet ministers oppose the Prime Minister they could be sacked at the next reshuffle.**

This may mean that ministers are reluctant to oppose the views of the Prime Minister.

The United Kingdom Parliament

At present, the UK Parliament has 72 MPs (out of 659) representing constituencies in Scotland. Elections must take place at least once every five years though the Prime Minister has the power to call an election before that time has elapsed. Westminster elections are decided using the 'First Past the Post' system.

Since the opening of the Scottish Parliament in 1999, Westminster MPs have dealt with a more restricted portfolio. Some of the important 'reserved' functions which are still dealt with at Westminster include defence, national economic issues, welfare benefits and foreign relations. Other areas are the responsibility of the Scottish Parliament.

The role of Parliament

◆ **Making new laws**

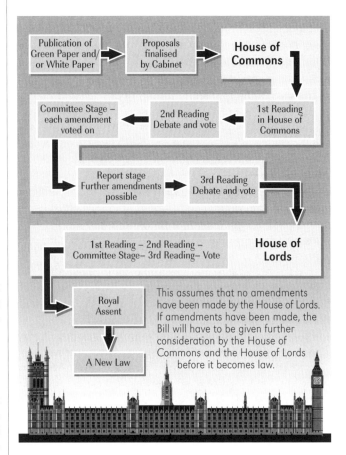

◆ **Controlling finance**

The House of Commons has absolute responsibility for financial matters. Each year, the Chancellor of the Exchequer presents his Budget statement to the House of Commons, outlining the government's plans for raising and spending money.

◆ **Scrutinising government**

The government has to explain its policies and there are opportunities to criticise the government. Scrutiny is carried out by Select Committees, at Question Time, during debates including Adjournment Debates and on Opposition Days.

What are the powers of backbench MPs?

All MPs who are not promoted are referred to as backbench MPs.

◆ **Backbench MPs can question ministers at Question Time**

MPs can question the Prime Minister or other ministers on issues of concern to them. A backbench MP could take the chance to question the Prime Minister about his handling of the war in Iraq.

◆ **Backbench MPs can lobby ministers**

This provides backbench MPs with the opportunity to influence government policy. If, for example, they are unhappy with government policy on the environment, they could speak to the minister and ask him/her to consider some alternatives.

◆ **Backbench MPs can vote on a range of different issues**

MPs have the power to vote in favour of or against government policy. If the government only has a small majority, then it is easier for MPs to exert pressure on it. MPs can also vote against the government if they feel strongly enough. When the present government proposed top-up university fees, a large number of Labour MPs voted against the proposals reducing the government's majority to 5.

◆ **Backbench MPs can introduce a Private Member's Bill**

If an MP wanted to ban fox hunting in England and Wales, it would be possible for the member to draft a bill which could go all the way through Parliament. In 1999, Tony Benn MP introduced a Private Member's Bill to reduce the powers of the Prime Minister.

What are the limitations on the powers of backbench MPs?

◆ **Backbench MPs may find it very difficult to influence government policy**

If the government has a large majority in Parliament, the influence of individual backbench MPs will be reduced accordingly. Labour won the election in 2001 with a majority of 167. An individual MP will find it very difficult to challenge the government in such a situation.

◆ **Backbench MPs may be faced with a conflict of interest**

Voters in a backbench MP's constituency may want one thing and the government another. The present government wants to build a number of new nuclear power stations and would expect all of their MPs to support them. However, voters and indeed party members from the constituency may not like such a development in their area because of fears about health.

◆ **Whips can influence the way in which backbench MPs vote**

If MPs are told to vote with the government (a three line whip) and ignore this, they can be disciplined and all party support withdrawn. The whips may also keep information on MPs that can be used to ensure they vote in a particular way. This may be seen as a form of blackmail.

◆ **There are 659 MPs in the House of Commons**

This makes it difficult for individual MPs to influence the government. MPs have few opportunities to talk in debates, lobby ministers or speak to the Prime Minister.

The Mass Media

Does the mass media shape political attitudes?

Arguments for

◆ The number of floating voters has increased and so the capacity of the media to influence opinions on issues is enhanced. In the past, people were more likely to be loyal to the same party throughout their lives.

◆ If political parties did not think that the mass media could influence political attitudes, then they would not spend time trying to influence the media. All political parties employ spin-doctors to encourage the media to represent their party's image in a positive manner. Alistair Campbell, who was the Prime Minister's Director of Communications until 2003, was one of the best-known spin-doctors.

◆ A large number of people read papers on a regular basis. If you read papers that are taking a political stance, then the chances are that they will influence your attitudes on a number of key issues.

◆ With the introduction of 24-hour television, it is possible to influence people at times which would have been missed in the past. Voters can 'catch' the news whenever they want.

◆ Political parties still put a great deal of time, effort and money into party election broadcasts.

Arguments against

◆ Newspapers do not influence political attitudes, as readers mostly buy papers that support their own views. If you support Labour, you are more likely to buy the Guardian but if you support the Conservatives, you are more likely to buy the Telegraph. Only 36% of Sun readers voted in the 2001 election.

◆ There are many other factors that are significant in shaping political attitudes – your socio-economic background, where you live, your standard of living, your race, your gender and your religion.

◆ At election time, many voters try to avoid the saturation coverage. They will not read newspaper articles or watch television programmes about politics. Also, more and more people are not turning out to vote. This suggests that the mass media are not shaping political attitudes in any significant way.

Turnout at UK General Elections

1945	72.7%
1950	84.0%
1951	82.5%
1955	76.7%
1959	78.8%
1964	77.1%
1966	75.8%
1970	72.0%
1974 (Feb)	78.5%
1974 (Oct)	72.8%
1979	76.0%
1983	72.7%
1987	75.3%
1992	77.7%
1997	71.5%
2001	58.2%

THE NATURE OF POLITICAL COMMUNICATIONS

The mass media's position as being the single largest source of political information in the modern world puts it in an important position within the political process. Its influence and its potential to be manipulated by political organisations raise the question of whether the mass media has a positive or negative effect on democratic politics.

Media organisations would principally include television and radio stations, newspapers, news agencies, and magazine and book publishers, film producers and studios and internet information providers.

Political organisations include government, political parties, public institutions, pressure and interest groups, and even terrorist organisations.

Pressure Groups

Some pressure groups are more effective than others. The degree to which a pressure group is effective may be influenced by factors like the number of members, level of expertise, resources available, leadership, finances, if they are insider or outsider groups and the level of media/government interest.

What methods are used by pressure groups?

Shock tactics
Demonstrations
Lobbying MPs/MSPs
Strikes or boycotts
Destruction of GM crops by Greenpeace
Posters and leaflets (mail shots)
Presentations at schools
Blocked roads – fuel protestors
Websites
Petitions
Advertising
Surveys
Riots by anti-capitalist groups at World Bank meetings
Go slows – fuel demonstrations
Media coverage

To what extent are pressure groups undemocratic?

◆ **Some pressure groups have substantial resources and well-off members**
Pressure groups with money will be able to do more than groups which have less money. Thus the success of a campaign may have more to do with finance than the quality of the arguments. This may mean that groups such as the Countryside Alliance have more media success than anti-fox hunting groups.

◆ **Some pressure groups may break the law**
Some groups that oppose animal testing (Animal Aid) may break-in to laboratories and release the animals used for testing. Not only may this cause a lot of resentment among workers involved but also may result in conflict with the authorities.

◆ **Pressure groups have little influence over government decisions**
Even though pressure groups may enjoy widespread support, they may have little influence over government decisions. Most consultation between pressure groups and the government happens behind closed doors. This means it is difficult to assess the extent of the influence of insider groups. Outsider groups will have little influence in this process.

◆ **Many pressure groups are not democratic in themselves**
The decision-making process within pressure groups often ignores the wishes of the membership. Leaders are often appointed for life, making it difficult for members to change policy or make the leadership accountable.

To what extent are pressure groups democratic?

◆ **Insider pressure groups may provide information that will help government to make informed decisions on new policies**
For example, the Automobile Association is often consulted about proposed changes to transport policy in the UK. Policies that develop from this process will be based on the latest evidence and will have a greater chance of gaining public support.

◆ **Pressure groups can prevent government pursuing policies that may be unpopular or ineffective**
The anti-poll tax campaign in the 1980s was successful in getting the government to change a system of local taxation that was making poor people poorer.

◆ **Pressure groups allow minority views to be expressed in a more effective manner**
Often the views of small groups are ignored because they do not impact on the majority of people in the population.

◆ **Pressure groups encourage individuals to take a much more active part in the decision-making process**
Pressure groups are more likely to be involved in single issues. If people actively participate, it must be good for democracy. For example, more than 8 million people are members of trade unions. This gives them the opportunity to campaign for the rights of workers.

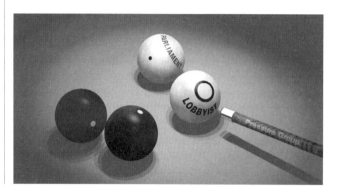

Politics in the United Kingdom
The Government of Scotland

WHAT THE SQA SAYS WILL BE IN THE EXAM

(a) Decision-making in Scotland: structure and functions of Scottish Parliament; local government; Scottish Office and government departments and agencies.

(b) Relationship between Scottish Parliament and UK Parliament: distribution of powers; conflicts between them.

(c) Relationship between Scottish Parliament and local government in Scotland: distribution of power, conflicts between them.

Scotland's Local Government

Scotland has 29 mainland and 3 island local authorities or councils. Although efforts were made at the 1996 reorganisation of local authorities to set up councils of roughly equal population bases, there are considerable differences in population size among the Scottish councils. A council, such as Glasgow, with a large number of people concentrated into a relatively small urban area, has to tackle its service delivery in a very different way from smaller councils such as the Borders which has a number of small communities spread over a wide geographical area.

Councils have responsibility for a wide range of service provision including education, housing, roads, social work, planning, leisure and recreation and refuse collection. Councils still play a major part in our daily lives, but for several years now their power has been waning.

For many years, council staff delivered council services. In recent years, many councils have begun to pay 'outside' firms to do what used to be council work – for example, catering organisations often now provide school meals or clean council buildings. Although councils may still employ their own staff to deliver a service, they must show that it is 'best value' – that an outside firm could not do it more cost-effectively. This, in effect, has meant fewer council employees and less council control.

Council Services

◆ **Some council services are mandatory**
Councils must make them available, e.g. nursery, primary and secondary schools.
◆ **Some council services are permissive**
Councils are allowed to make them available, e.g. leisure centres.
◆ **Some council services are discretionary**
Councils may make them available e.g. arts events.

Finance

Local authority finance has been a cause of disagreement between councils and central government for many years.

Sources of Local Government Income

For Capital Expenditure

Borrowing from Banks

Public Private Partnerships (PPP)

European Union

For Revenue Expenditure

Grants from Central Government

Non-Domestic/Business Rates

Council Tax

Charges for Selected Services

For Housing Expenditure

Council House Rents

Central Government

Grants

The two most important sources of money for councils are, firstly, money raised locally through the council tax, and, secondly, an annual grant from the Scottish Executive. This gives central government the power to restrict council spending, both through limiting government grants and by discouraging local authorities from raising their council tax by too much at a time. Also, central government sets the level of business rates paid by private companies, reducing councils' power still further. Councils must also seek approval for their spending plans. Less money means less power.

Local and Central Government

Despite the fact that the Labour Party – especially in Scotland – holds a dominant position in local government, there has been little sign that either the Labour Government in London or the Scottish Executive has any intention of restoring power to local councils. Perhaps the most telling reduction in the power of councils has come in the area of housing.

Housing

There have been massive changes in the provision of council housing. At one time, more than 50% of Scots occupied council houses – this gave councils and councillors a huge degree of influence. Over the last twenty years, council tenants have been able to buy their homes at a discount price. This 'right to buy' has reduced the stock of housing available to councils. Councils have also been left with huge housing debts and few resources to spend on renovating the houses they have left.

Scottish Executive policies have pushed councils towards selling off their housing to housing organisations not connected to the council. At the same time, money for new social housing has been channelled towards housing associations rather than towards councils. Housing providers are expected to involve the private sector in funding the building of new houses. So, although local councils still have substantial responsibilities in, for example, developing housing strategies and in housing homeless people, they are, increasingly, losing control of their housing stock.

In April 2002, 58% of the tenants of Glasgow Council voted to change their landlord from the council to the Glasgow Housing Association. This decision is likely to be the subject of continuing debate and even legal argument.

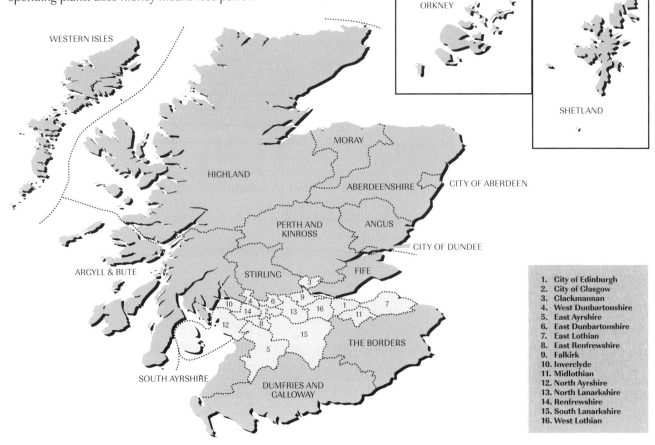

1. City of Edinburgh
2. City of Glasgow
3. Clackmannan
4. West Dunbartonshire
5. East Ayrshire
6. East Dunbartonshire
7. East Lothian
8. East Renfrewshire
9. Falkirk
10. Inverclyde
11. Midlothian
12. North Ayrshire
13. North Lanarkshire
14. Renfrewshire
15. South Lanarkshire
16. West Lothian

Education

The Scottish Executive influences council priorities in order to meet its own objectives. The Executive may offer more money for education but only if councils spend it in a way specified by the government. Councils, for example, may receive extra money from the Executive but only if they agree to spend it on areas specified by the Executive. This is termed ' ring-fencing'. Organisations such as school boards have been set up. Their priorities are often at odds with those of their local council.

Council Elections

Council membership is decided by elections held at fixed times. 'First Past the Post' is the electoral system used, although a change to proportional representation is under active consideration by the Scottish Executive. This move is being opposed by many local government politicians, particularly Labour politicians, who anticipate that it may lead to the Labour Party losing control of some councils. Though a significant number of independent councillors remains, most Scottish local councils are run by political party groupings.

The Scottish Parliament

The Scottish Parliament in Edinburgh has 129 MSPs elected under a form of proportional representation called 'the additional member system'. 73 MSPs are directly elected to specific constituencies with the remainder being 'party list' MSPs. The parliamentary term lasts four years and the First Minister does not have the option of calling an election earlier than that.

'Reserved' Powers

- ◆ The Constitution
- ◆ Defence
- ◆ Foreign Affairs
- ◆ Energy Policy
- ◆ Most Economic Policy
- ◆ Immigration and Asylum Seekers
- ◆ Aspects of Medical Ethics
- ◆ Social Security
- ◆ Most Taxation/Fiscal Policy

Some Key 'Devolved' Powers

- ◆ Health
- ◆ Education
- ◆ Rural Development, including Agriculture and Fisheries
- ◆ Enterprise, Lifelong Learning and Economic Development
- ◆ Justice, the Courts and the Police
- ◆ Local Government
- ◆ The Environment and some Transport Policy
- ◆ Housing and Social Work
- ◆ Social Inclusion
- ◆ Sport, Culture and the Arts

Additional Member Vote System		56 MSPs					
	Highlands & Islands	2	2	2	1		
	North East Scotland	3	2	1	1		
	Mid Scotland & Fife	3	2	1	1		
	West of Scotland	3	2	1	1		
	Glasgow	2	2	1	1	1	
	Central Scotland	3	1	1	1	1	1
	Lothians	2	2	1	1	1	
	South of Scotland	3	2	1	1		

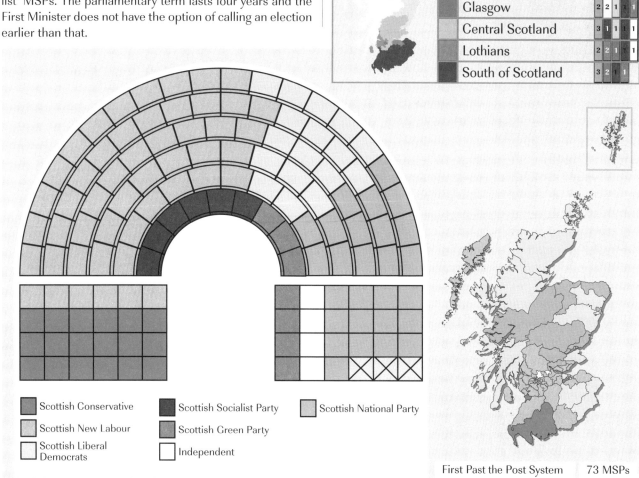

- Scottish Conservative
- Scottish New Labour
- Scottish Liberal Democrats
- Scottish Socialist Party
- Scottish Green Party
- Independent
- Scottish National Party

First Past the Post System   73 MSPs

The Scottish Parliament has the authority to set policy on a wide range of issues including education, health, agriculture and transport. In these areas, the Scottish Parliament may choose to adopt a different approach from that applying to, say, England. This has already caused strains between Holyrood and Westminster. The Scottish Parliament has, for example, abolished university tuition fees and is committed to providing free care for the elderly. These benefits are not available in England. It also has the power to raise or lower the rate of income tax by up to 3p in the pound.

The elections to the Scottish Parliament in 1999 and again in 2003 gave none of the parties an overall majority. A coalition government involving the dominant party, the Labour Party, and the Liberal Democrats, was the result in both instances.

The Scottish National Party was the second largest party with the Conservatives, the Scottish Socialist Party, the Green Party and some independents also represented. Supporters of proportional representation regarded the results as a vindication of the system, and noted that the Scottish Conservatives, the most committed opponents of PR, had to rely on it for many of its representatives.

Holyrood and Westminster

The setting up of the Scottish Parliament has led to demands that the number of MPs allocated to Scotland should be reduced to reflect the transfer of many areas of work from Westminster to Holyrood. MPs representing constituencies in England have also queried the logic of MPs from Scotland voting on matters which exclusively affect the rest of the United Kingdom, i.e. England and Wales, while MPs representing the rest of the UK have no vote on matters which are the responsibility of Holyrood. This is often termed 'the West Lothian Question'. Other tensions relate to the level of block grant which Westminster allocates to Holyrood to run Scotland's business.

The need for a Secretary of State for Scotland and a Scotland Office has also been queried as an unnecessary expense and a source of political tension between the personalities involved. The post of Secretary of State for Scotland is currently filled by the Secretary of State for Transport, Alistair Darling.

What does the Scottish Parliament do?

The Departments of the Scottish Office (pre 1999)
Agriculture, Environment and Fisheries Department
Home Department
Education and Industry Department
Health Department
Development Department

The Departments of the Scottish Executive (post 1999)
Corporate Services
Development
Education
Enterprise and Lifelong Learning
Finance
Health
Justice
Rural Affairs
Executive Secretariat

The Scottish Parliament in operation

The 129 MSPs elect a Presiding Officer ('chairperson') from among the elected MSPs. This is currently George Reid. The majority political party - or parties – form the Scottish Executive. The MSPs elect a First Minister – at present Jack McConnell – who is the equivalent of the Prime Minister in the UK Parliament and whose appointment is also approved by the Queen. The First Minister appoints ministers to run the various departments. Junior ministers may also be appointed. There are also two Law Officers, the Lord Advocate (Colin Boyd QC) and the Solicitor General (Eilish Angiolini) who are appointed by the Queen on the recommendation of the First Minister.

The Scottish Parliament started officially on 12th May 1999. Each parliament lasts for four years. Note that while a successful vote of 'no confidence' in the executive can bring about an earlier General Election, the First Minister does not, as the UK Prime Minister does, have the option of calling an earlier election.

What are the functions of the Scottish Parliament?

The Standing Orders which regulate the sittings of the Scottish Parliament are complex.

A Typical Week in the Scottish Parliament
Monday
MSPs on Constituency business.
Tuesday
Committees meet in Edinburgh or at various venues around Scotland.
Wednesday
Morning: Committee sessions. *Lunchtime*: Party meetings. *Afternoon*: Plenary session in main chamber.
Thursday
Plenary session including oral questions during the afternoon.
Friday
MSPs on Constituency business.

As at Westminster, a great deal of important work is done by parliamentary committees which have between five and fifteen members. Committees are politically balanced to reflect the composition of Parliament as a whole. Meetings are held in public, can be held anywhere in Scotland and can invite any person to attend as a witness. Key committees include:

The Mandatory Committees

- Procedures
- Standards
- Finance
- Audit
- European
- Equal Opportunities
- Public Petitions
- Subordinate Legislation

Other committees, known as Subject Committees, can be established by Parliament to look at specific areas of concern, including committees for Health and Community Care and Rural Development.

The Scottish Executive brings most proposed legislation to Parliament, though one of the most contentious measures – to control hunting with dogs – was brought by Mike Watson as a Private Member's Bill. Committees can also bring forward proposals.

A Bill goes through three stages.

Pre-legislative Scrutiny

Consultation and checks to see if the Parliament is entitled to consider the particular issue at stake.

✓   ✗   🗑

Stage 1

Consideration of the general principles of the bill (overall, is it a good idea or a bad idea?) and a decision (vote) by MSPs on whether it should proceed.

✓   ✗   🗑

Stage 2

A detailed examination of the bill, line-by-line, and taking evidence from witnesses.

This stage is normally undertaken by one or more committees, one of which will be the Lead Committee for the bill.

Stage 3

Final consideration of the bill and any changes suggested and a decision on whether to pass or reject it.

✓   ✗   🗑

Further possible checks by Scottish and UK Law Officers and the Secretary of State for Scotland, which might lead to resubmission and reconsideration.

Submission by the Presiding Officer to the Sovereign for Royal Assent.

Receiving Royal Assent

At this stage the Bill becomes an Act.

How MSPs can raise matters in Parliament

Executive Accountability to Parliament
Oral and Written questions
Making statements in the Chamber
Leading debates in plenary session
Scrutiny of departmental expenditure
Giving evidence to committees

The Scottish Parliament – Matters Arising

◆ The media helped to give the Scottish Parliament a positive start. Since then some Holyrood parliamentarians have felt that the Scottish media have been more carping than constructive. Newspapers have, for example, devoted a great deal of space to Mike Watson's 'ban on hunting' bill, and to issues around members' expenses rather than, for example, to the huge amount of committee work going on at Holyrood. Again, there has been a focus on members who have other jobs outside Holyrood. Some feel that this reflects a long-standing anti-devolution stance in some newspapers – they do not intend to view Holyrood in a positive light.

◆ The death of Donald Dewar in 2000 was a blow to the developing Parliament. Dewar was a great supporter of devolution and was the First Minister in the Scottish Executive. Many MSPs were new to parliamentary politics, and, while Holyrood was 'finding its feet', the presence of a politician of such substance and experience was invaluable.

◆ Dewar's successor, Henry McLeish, was forced to resign over financial matters relating to his constituency office. McLeish's own successor, Jack McConnell, had to survive revelations about his private life before winning office. Some commentators discerned tensions in Scottish Labour after McConnell's leadership victory. A 'cabinet reshuffle' in the Scottish Executive suggested that their suspicions were justified.

◆ 'Turf wars' have broken out between constituency MSPs, and 'list' MSPs, with some constituency members resenting what they regarded as so-called 'interference' in their patch by list MSPs belonging to other parties.

◆ There has been some disappointment that, despite the opportunity for a fresh approach to politics, 'Westminster' style politicking has carried over into the Scottish Parliament. Supporters of the Scottish Parliament would, however, point out that the LibDem Depute First Minister was able, with the agreement and support of Labour members, to become Acting First Minister. It is extremely unlikely that this could happen at Westminster. Similarly, MSPs elected the Tory, Murray Tosh, to the post of Depute Presiding Officer, inflicting an unexpected defeat on Labour's Cathy Peattie, Jack McConnell's choice.

◆ The Parliament has had to deal with some unexpected contentious issues. The 2000 SQA debacle led to media criticism of Sam Galbraith, the Education Minister at the time. Nevertheless, the matter was decisively dealt with by Galbraith's successor, Jack McConnell. Similarly, the outbreak of Foot and Mouth disease in 2001 left the Executive in great difficulty. Most commentators feel that it was dealt with more satisfactorily in Scotland by Ross Finnie, the Agriculture Minister, than it was in other parts of the UK.

◆ Health issues continue to dog the Scottish Executive. Waiting lists, 'dirty' hospitals and staff problems (e.g. at the Beatson cancer facility in Glasgow) have all provided targets for attack by opposition politicians.

◆ Initiatives such as the abolition of student tuition fees and the provision of free care for the elderly – not available in other parts of the UK – have perhaps not had the praise they deserve.

◆ There is a view that there are too many MSPs in Holyrood, although plans to reduce the numbers in line with a proposed reduction in the number of Scottish Westminster MPs have been vigorously opposed by the Parliament.

◆ Tensions arose between the Holyrood Parliament and the UK Parliament when there was uncertainty over the possible building of new nuclear power stations. George Foulkes, the Westminster minister at the time, argued that the final decision on UK energy policy must lie with London. MSPs disagreed, and demanded clarification. The Prime Minister came down on the side of Holyrood.

◆ The cost of the new Parliament building at Holyrood has soared, giving opponents a further supply of ammunition to criticise the devolution settlement. An initial figure of £50 million spiralled to around £400 million, with even experts unable to agree on what the final amount might be. The Fraser Inquiry has revealed a considerable degree of concern about the reasons for the escalation in the cost of the Parliament building.

◆ There have been tensions between Holyrood and local councils. In housing, for example, the Scottish Executive has put pressure on councils to transfer their council houses into the control of alternative landlords. Many councillors do not agree with the policy in principle, but feel that the financial incentives available to councils which transfer their stock cannot be ignored. Again, the Scottish Executive has made money available for the 'rationalisation' – seen by many as a code word for closures - of schools through Public Private Partnership finance schemes. Councils may not like the system, but, if they want to repair crumbling school buildings, they have to accept it. Many councillors, regardless of party affiliation, did not like the reliance on private finance, feeling that it was wrong in principle and not a cost-effective option in practice. Eventually, early in 2002, two councils, West Dunbartonshire and Falkirk, neither of them Labour-controlled, challenged Holyrood on this issue. In 2003, East Lothian Council experienced major problems when Ballast UK, their PPP partner, went into liquidation.

Politics in the United Kingdom
Political Parties and their Policies

WHAT THE SQA SAYS WILL BE IN THE EXAM

(a) Political parties – ideology, membership, organisation, internal decision-making, electoral success.

(b) The nature/role of conflict and consensus: broad differences and changes in party ideologies; influences on party policies.

(c) Party policies on taxation, law and order, employment, private and public ownership/control, health, education – trends and differences.

Political parties in the UK consist of groups of people who share an ideology – 'what they stand for' – and a desire to win political power so that their ideology becomes dominant in the running of the country. An ideology consists of a set of attitudes, especially political attitudes, towards issues such as crime, education, health care, defence and taxation. In our democracy, political parties seek to persuade voters to support them by expressing their ideologies through their policies.

Party Ideologies

The three main parties all have ideologies which are recognisable on the 'left-right' political spectrum. As well as the major parties, the other parties represented in the Commons, such as the Scottish National Party, Plaid Cymru and the parties based in Northern Ireland have unique, locally important, ideologies relating to sovereignty, which mean that they will never form the government of the UK.

Differences between the ideologies of the leading parties are no longer as distinct as they once were.

The Labour Party

'New Labour' advocates values such as social justice, strong communities, reward for hard work, decency and rights matched by responsibilities. Although still a party of equality and inclusiveness, and emphasising the importance of improving public services, Labour now leans less towards state intervention and publicly – run services as a means of promoting those values than it used to emphasise. Again, Labour won an election on a 'no rise in Income Tax policy – a departure from a previously held insistence that redistribution of wealth was a prerequisite for a fair society. Labour has, notably, made no attempt to modify policies adopted by previous Conservative governments on council house 'right to buy', on measures to curb trade unions or on Private Finance Initiatives. Labour has endorsed private prisons and the privatisation of air traffic control. When Railtrack failed, Stephen Byers, the Transport Secretary, was unwilling to nationalise Britain's railways.

The Conservative Party

The Conservative Party has always been less rigidly ideological than Labour. Their approach derived from a belief in self-reliance, enterprise and freedom of choice within a framework of law and order. This outlook led to policies based on low taxation and minimal state intervention. Until the advent of 'New Labour', the Tories were consistently successful in winning elections – from 1950 to 2000 the Tories were in power in Westminster for twice as long as Labour.

After two consecutive election defeats, however, the Conservatives have had to rethink. The importance placed on the NHS by the public has caused them to modify their previous emphasis on private health care, and to undertake to guarantee the NHS. Labour has adopted policies on, for example, asylum seekers, law and order, private finance and immigration which have stolen the Tories' thunder.

The choice of Michael Howard as their new leader may lead to a Conservative Party which is more aggressive in its scrutiny of the Labour Government and in its advocacy of core Conservative values.

The Liberal Democratic Party

Liberal Democrat ideology is based on individual freedom and equality of opportunity within a community framework. They believe that democracy is best served if decisions are made at the most local level possible, and that everyone's vote should count. The Lib Dems' most distinctive policies have been their demand for proportional representation and their view that income tax should be increased to pay for education. They are also the most strongly pro-European party and have pursued 'green' policies such as the phasing out of nuclear power. The Lib Dems were seen as the driving force behind the Scottish Executive's commitment to free care for the elderly.

Membership of the Two Main Parties

Although the relationship is less reliable than it used to be, social class is still a factor in membership of political parties. While many recruits to 'New Labour' were middle class professionals, it still has, by far, more working class adherents than the other parties. This has caused tension in the party, with some 'Old Labour' members fearing that traditional party values were being sacrificed to accommodate 'yuppie' aspirations, and worrying that support, particularly in Scotland, where 'Old Labour' ideals are still strong, may slip away to the Scottish National Party or to the Scottish Socialist Party.

Conservatives are still associated with the middle and upper social classes, although it has often been pointed out that the Tories can only win elections if a substantial number of working class people vote for them. Despite movement towards reform, the House of Lords still has a built-in Tory majority, reflecting the social class balance of the party.

Despite ideological differences, leading politicians of the main parties often appear to have similar social and educational backgrounds – private schools, Oxbridge and the legal profession provide a number of MPs which is out of all proportion to their numbers in society as a whole. MPs have often been described as 'middle class, middle aged, male and white'.

Party Organisation

The Labour Party

Despite their importance to our democracy, the parties themselves are not run entirely democratically.

Labour has, on the face of it, a party structure which allows 'grass-roots' involvement.

- ◆ A network of local branches holds regular meetings which can be used as 'sounding-boards' by the party leadership. Branches can have an input into the selection of Labour local council election candidates.

- ◆ The constituency Labour Party consists of the branches in a constituency. The constituency party sends delegates to conference and can help select parliamentary candidates.

- ◆ Labour also runs informal local and regional policy forums which, together with the National Policy Forum and various Policy Commissions, prepare policy papers for consideration by the party as a whole.

- ◆ The National Executive Committee, made up of representatives from each section of the party, sets the party's objectives and supervises the running of the party.

- ◆ The Annual Conference decides on the policy framework and sets party rules.

Some commentators have pointed out that, despite the above, the parliamentary leadership has increased its power at the expense of the ordinary members. There have been accusations of interference in local selection processes. Some choices are not made on 'one person, one vote', but by an 'electoral college' system.

Some Labour members feel that the party has placed too much reliance on unaccountable advisers, 'spin-doctors' and focus groups at the expense of the ordinary party member. In response, the party leadership would point to two consecutive election victories.

Politics in the United Kingdom

The Conservative Party

Although they also have the local branch at the core of their organisation, the Tories have always operated in a less formal and structured way than Labour. Former leader William Hague decentralised the party in order to improve communication between the ordinary party members and the leadership.

Under the overall supervision of the party's governing board, the core unit is the constituency association, which recruits members, selects candidates and puts forward representatives to area committees. The performance of constituency associations is monitored by the board – elected from the membership - which can, in exceptional circumstances, intervene in the affairs of associations. Members take part directly in the election of the party leader, and may attend twice-yearly National Conservative Conventions and the Annual Conference. Issues discussed at party conferences have tended to reflect the preferences of the leadership rather than the grass roots. Tory conferences are carefully orchestrated celebrations of party unity, though disagreement over the European Union, for example, is now proving regularly troublesome.

The organisation of the two main parties

	Labour	Conservative
Local Branch	*	*
Constituency Association	*	*
Local / Regional Policy Forum		*
Area Committees	*	
National Policy Forum	*	
National Executive Committee	*	
Annual Conference	*	*

Party Policies

Conservative Party

Tax and the Economy

- cut fuel tax by 6p a litre
- local referendums before large increase in council tax
- lower taxes for businesses, families, savers, pensioners and motorists
- cut public spending by £8 billion to finance tax cuts
- public spending not to outstrip the growth of the economy
- no more "stealth" taxes
- less regulation for business
- keep the pound
- reform tax for charities
- new married couples allowance
- increase the basic state pension
- establish Regeneration Companies to revitalise inner cities and housing estates
- cut business rates for rural shops, pubs, garages and village post offices
- privatise Channel Four

Education

- freedom for headteachers to run schools
- power for parents to change management of failing schools
- endowment for universities

Law and Order

- increase police numbers
- less police bureaucracy
- take persistent young offenders off the streets
- criminals to serve the sentence given by the court
- more rights for victims
- a 'safe haven, not a soft touch', on asylum
- new police powers to deal with drug abuse

Health

- increase NHS funding
- allow patients and GPs to choose which hospital is best for treatment
- remove tax penalty on private medical insurance
- guaranteed limits on waiting times
- protect the savings and homes of those needing long term care

Labour Party

Tax and the Economy

- no rise in the top or basic rate of income tax
- mortgages as low as possible
- low inflation
- sound public finances
- increase minimum wage to £4.20 an hour
- bring in a new trust fund for every child at birth
- increase spending on transport by 20% a year for next 3 years
- create an Integrated Child Credit, and Pension Credit
- establish an Employment First interview for claimants
- integrate Benefits Agency and Employment Service
- recruit more staff to drive up public service standards

Education

- increase spending on education by more than 5% each year for 3 years
- 10,000 more teachers
- radically improve secondary schools
- diversify state schools
- direct more money through headteachers
- give more freedom to successful schools
- expand childcare places to provide for 1.6 million children

Law and Order

- an extra £1.6bn a year to be spent on police by 2003-04
- 6,000 extra police recruits
- overhaul sentencing to provide tougher punishment
- introduce a victims' bill of rights
- register criminal drug dealers
- deal with asylum abuse

Health

- increase spending on health by an average of 6% each year for 3 years
- 20,000 more nurses, 10,000 more doctors
- decentralise power to Primary Care Trusts
- ensure booked appointments by 2005
- cut maximum waiting times by end of 2005
- create specially-built surgical units to cut delays

Liberal Democratic Party

Tax and the Economy

- a penny on the basic rate of income tax to fund £3.5bn education programme
- 50% top rate of tax on earnings over £100,000, generating £4.6bn
- changes to Capital Gains Tax, to raise £2bn
- single pensioner's basic pension up £5, by £10 for those over 75, and £15 for the over-80s, couples up £8, £18 and £28, respectively (the party costs its pension proposals at £2.9bn a year)
- free off-peak local travel for pensioners and the severely disabled
- half price travel for students under 19 at all times
- local authorities allowed to raise bonds to finance public transport projects
- workplace and out of town shopping centre parking charges to cut congestion
- abolish vehicle tax for small cars and motorbikes
  (the party costed its transport proposals at £500m annually)

Education

- cut average primary school classes to 25 by recruiting 12,500 new primary school teachers
- recruit 5,000 new secondary school teachers
- abolish university tuition fees
- cut bureaucracy and red tape for teachers
  (the party costed its education proposals at £3.5bn a year)

Law and Order

- police numbers up 6,000 on the year 2000
- part-time community officers to rise by 2,000 on last year
- recruit traffic wardens, park-keepers and others to work with police in a Community Safety Force, coordinated by local authorities
- more police units to tackle 'hate crime'
- extended prison education programme
- Royal Commission on Drugs
- victims able to make personal post-conviction, pre-sentence statement to courts
- fast track applications for asylum-seekers held in detention centres
- end discrimination in the immigration and asylum system
  (the party costed its law and order proposals at £250m annually)

Health

- 27,500 nurses and midwives and 4,600 doctors to be recruited by 2005
- 10,000 more hospital beds to be created by the same time
- nurses' annual pay to rise by an average £1,000 - those on lower salaries to get more
- free NHS dental and eye checks to be restored for all adults
- a new Pharmaceuticals Agency to keep down the health service drugs bill
- new screening equipment to allow same day diagnosis and treatment
- doctors to test for diseases such as HIV, Aids and TB at their surgeries
- all patients needing surgery or an appointment with a consultant to be given a firm date as soon as they are diagnosed
  (the party costed this at £3bn a year, and estimated that its Pharmaceuticals Agency will save around £1bn a year)

Scottish National Party

Tax and the Economy

- build a modern transport and telecommunications infrastructure
- the complete abolition of tuition fees
- an intensive campaign of selling Scotland to the world
- £260m for health, education and crime
- a Scottish fund for future generations to make the wealth of Scotland work for the people of Scotland
- a Scottish trust for public investment to invest more, at less cost, in schools, hospitals and transport
- a comprehensive review of taxation – immediate 10p a gallon fuel tax cut and a new 45p-tax band for those earning more than £100,000

Education

- reduce primary one, two and three class sizes to 18
- a moratorium on further change, until the establishment of an education convention
- end the publication of selective information and league tables for schools
- introduce a major programme of school investment and repair

Law and Order

- employ 1,000 more police on Scotland's streets
- encourage greater parental responsibility – parents to be held responsible to victims of their children's crime
- tough action on sex offenders
- ensure that victims of crime should not become victims of the criminal justice system

Health

- end 'postcode treatment' of patients within the National Health Service
- supply free daily fruit for all children in primary schools
- remove charges for dental check-ups
- cut waiting times for inpatient treatment by half
- employ 1,500 more nurses
- free personal care for the elderly

Politics in the United Kingdom
The Electoral System, Voting and Political Attitudes

WHAT THE SQA SAYS WILL BE IN THE EXAM

(a) The UK and Scottish electoral systems and alternative systems: how they work; effects upon the distribution of power.

(b) Voting patterns, explanations of voting behaviour – social differentiation; national and regional variations; age; gender; ethnic background.

(c) The shaping of political attitudes (e.g. through the media).

What are the factors which influence voting behaviour?

Factor	Nature of influence	Characteristics
Social Context	Long Term	Social influences on voters include social class, age, gender, religion, region, family, friends and workplace colleagues.
Party Identification	Long Term	Voter's sense of attachment to a political party.
Attitudes	Long and Short Term	How a voter feels about political issues, the performance of government and the social values that society should have.
Voting Context	Short Term	Voter's perception of the purpose or meaning of the election.
Media Context	Short Term	Voter's exposure to political information from media sources such as newspapers and television.
Government & Political Party Actions	Long and Short Term	How the effects of government policy and the political parties directly impact upon the voter's everyday life.

The way people vote is influenced by a number of factors including where they live; their socio-economic background; their gender; their religion; the level of education; the ethnic group that they belong to; their age; the beliefs of the party; the leader of the party; the mass media. All of the above factors will influence voters to some extent.

1. Where people live – geographical factors

◆ Scotland, North of England and Wales tend to support Labour while the South of England tends to vote Conservative. In the 2001 election, only one Conservative MP was elected in Scotland. None were elected in Wales.

◆ Religious tensions in Northern Ireland mean that people do not vote for UK parties. You are much more likely to get support if you are a candidate for one of the Ulster-based nationalist or unionist parties.

2. Religion
Religion can influence voting behaviour. In the past in Scotland, Catholics were more likely to vote Labour and Protestants more likely to vote Conservative. Theorists would argue that this was due to the links with Northern Ireland. The Conservatives were called the Conservative and Unionist Party, reflecting their wish to keep Northern Ireland (as well as Scotland and Wales) part of the UK.

3. Education
In most developed countries, the more educated you are the more likely you are to vote at elections.

4. Socio-economic background
Many people would argue that socio-economic background was the main influence on voting behaviour in the UK. For decades, most working class people would vote Labour and most middle class people would vote Conservative. To some extent this may still be true. However, it is not as clear-cut today as it once was.

Class Percentages Voting Conservative, Labour and Liberal Democrat

	AB	C1	C2	DE
1992 General Election				
Conservative	56	52	38	30
Labour	20	25	41	50
Liberal Democrat	22	19	17	15
1997 General Election				
Conservative	42	26	25	21
Labour	31	47	54	61
Liberal Democrat	21	19	14	13
2001 General Election				
Conservative	40	35	29	27
Labour	33	39	47	50
Liberal Democrat	21	20	18	18

5. Race

Ethnic minorities are more likely to vote Labour. It could be argued that they feel that Labour is more willing to help minorities than the Conservatives. However, this trend is changing and more ethnic minorities are voting according to their socio-economic circumstances. Better off minorities are more likely to vote Conservative while unskilled are more likely to vote Labour.

6. Gender

In the 1992 election, women were more likely to vote Conservative. 44% of women voted Conservative compared to 41% of men. This changed in 1997, when Labour were able to attract more women voters. They were also able to select more women candidates and 101 female Labour MPs were elected. 47% of men and 47% of women voted Labour.

Women's Voting Preference (%) and Age at the 2001 General Election

	Labour	Conservative
18-24	44	21
25-34	57	19
35-54	43	21
55+	46	34

Source: British Election Study 2001

7. Age

Young people are more likely to vote Labour. It is thought that this comes from the perception that 'New Labour' has a more radical edge. Better-off older people are more likely to vote Conservative. This may be because Conservative voters are more likely to have a high standard of living and are likely to live longer on average.

8. Ideology

Voters will vote for parties and candidates who share the same ideas as themselves. Many people did not vote for Labour in the 1980s because they did not share their views on taxation and defence. Their policies changed and many more people were willing to support them in 1997 and 2001.

9. Leadership

Many commentators would argue that the personality of the leader has a significant influence on voting behaviour. In 2001, commentators argued that many people voted Labour because they trusted Labour (Tony Blair) more than the Conservatives.

Electoral Systems

The First Past the Post System (FPTP)

The First Past the Post voting system is used in the UK to elect members to the Westminster Parliament. It is also known as the Simple Majority System.

How does first past the post work?

◆ The UK is divided up into 659 areas (called constituencies) and one Member of Parliament (MP) is elected from each.

◆ The candidate who wins the largest number of votes in each constituency is elected as the MP.

◆ The party that receives the largest number of MPs is asked by the Queen to form the government.

What are the arguments in favour of the FPTP?

◆ The FPTP system has been used in the UK for many years. This would indicate that British voters and politicians are happy with the system as it stands. If it were unpopular, it would have been changed by now.

◆ Other systems, like the Additional Member System, are much more complicated and voters are not always certain why representatives have been elected.

◆ In FPTP, there is a strong link between the voter and the elected representative. One person is elected from each constituency and this makes it easier for citizens to contact their own representative if they have a problem. Under other systems such as the Party List, the Single Transferable Vote and the Additional Member System, it is much more difficult to work out whom to contact.

◆ FPTP usually provides one party with an overall majority which allows it to form the government. This means that the government can take difficult decisions that may be unpopular. In 2001, Labour won 413 seats out of 659. A majority of 167 means that the Labour Government was able to make difficult decisions and ensure that Parliament would support them. An example of this was the way in which Tony Blair was able to promise support to the USA after the 9/11 terrorist attacks on New York.

Analysis of the 2001 General Election

General Election Results: 1979-2001 (UK)

	Con	Lab	Lib(a)	PC/SNP	Other	Total
Share of vote (%)						
1979	43.9%	36.9%	13.8%	2.0%	3.4%	100.0%
1983	42.4%	27.6%	25.4%	1.5%	3.1%	100.0%
1987	42.2%	30.8%	22.6%	1.7%	2.7%	100.0%
1992	41.9%	34.4%	17.8%	2.3%	3.5%	100.0%
1997	30.7%	43.2%	16.8%	2.5%	6.8%	100.0%
2001	31.7%	40.7%	18.3%	2.5%	6.9%	100.0%
Seats won						
1979	339	268	11	4	13	635
1983	397	209	23	4	17	650
1987	375	229	22	6	18	650
1992	336	271	20	7	17	651
1997	165	418	46	10	20	659
2001	166	412	52	9	20	659
Votes (millions)						
1979	13.7	11.5	4.3	0.6	1.1	31.2
1983	13.0	8.5	7.8	0.5	1.0	30.7
1987	13.7	10.0	7.3	0.5	0.9	32.5
1992	14.1	11.6	6.0	0.8	1.2	33.6
1997	9.6	13.5	5.2	0.8	2.1	31.3
2001	8.4	10.7	4.8	0.7	1.8	26.4

(a) Liberal/SDP Alliance 1983-87; Liberal Democrats from 1992
Sources: British Electoral Facts: 1832-1999, Parliamentary Research Services; House of Commons Library data on disk

General election results

◆ Since 1945 both the Conservatives and Labour have been the largest party, in term of seats won, on eight occasions.

◆ The Conservatives' best result since 1945 in terms of seats was 1983 when they won 397. Their highest share of the vote was in 1955 when they polled 49.6%.

◆ Labour's 418 seats won in 1997 is their highest ever while their highest share since 1945 was 48.8% in 1951, an election that they lost.

◆ In the 2001 General Election, the Liberal Democrats increased their number of seats by six to 52, the most won since 1945 by the party or its predecessors.

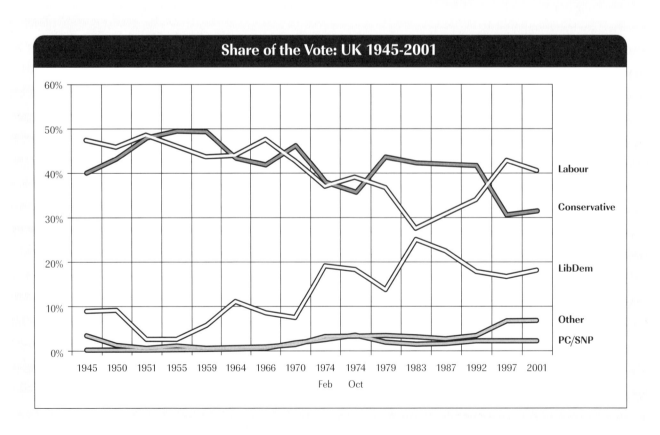

Share of the Vote: UK 1945-2001

What are the arguments against FPTP?

♦ In each constituency, the winning candidate is not required to win more than 50% of the votes cast. A candidate can usually win the seat with less than 50% of the vote.

It is clear to see why the FPTP system is often referred to as the 'winner takes all' system. There is nothing for the candidate who comes in second place.

The 2001 election result in the Galloway & Upper Nithsdale constituency shows this.

Candidate	Party	Votes	%
Peter Duncan	Conservative	12,222	34.0
Malcolm Fleming	SNP	12,148	33.8
Thomas Sloan	Labour	7,258	20.2
Neil Wallace	Liberal Democrat	3,698	10.3
Andy Harvey	Scottish Socialist	558	1.6
Majority		74	0.2
Turnout		35,914	68.1

♦ In the UK, the First Past the Post System has resulted in the domination of two parties, Labour and Conservative. They benefit disproportionately from FPTP, e.g. in 1983, Labour secured 209 seats in the Commons with 27.6% votes. In contrast, the Liberal Party won only 23 seats with 25.4% of the vote. This produced a result that did not relate to the percentage of votes received by each party and was therefore not reflective of the wishes of the voters.

In 2001, Labour won 413 seats with 40.7% of the vote while the Conservatives had 31.7% of the vote, but only won 166 seats. So for every percentage of the vote received, Labour won more than 10 seats but Conservatives only won 5.2.

♦ FPTP can also cause problems for the big two parties. In 1997, the Conservative Party received 17% of the vote in Scotland and 20% of the vote in Wales. However, this was not sufficient for the Conservatives to secure any seats at all. Many people would argue that their votes were wasted. This undermines the idea that all votes should be of equal value. If you live in a safe Labour seat but are a Conservative voter you may think that there is no point in taking part in the election because your vote will not make any difference. This is not the case with most types of proportional representation.

♦ If you are a floating voter in a marginal constituency, your vote will be very important. A small change in support could mean the difference between winning and losing. In the 1997 election, it was estimated that the parties targeted 66,000 floating voters in marginal constituencies whose votes could make the difference between success and failure.

♦ Voter turnout is falling. In 2001, in the Liverpool River constituency, only 34.1% of the electorate turned out to vote. In the country as a whole, the figure was only 58%.

Proportional Representation

There are a number of different types of voting system that that come under the heading of proportional representation.

The Party List System

How does it work?

Each party draws up a list of candidates. At the top of the list are those who are regarded as important to a party or who have influence in a party. The further down a list a candidate appears, the less likely he or she is to be elected. Under this system, people vote for a party not for a person. If a party gets 40% of the votes, then the top 40% on their list will be elected.

Arguments for the Party List System

♦ **Proportionality**
This is a very proportional system. If a party receives 10% of the vote, it will get 10% of the seats. No votes are wasted and each vote has equal value.

♦ **Ease of understanding**
This is probably the most straightforward system of proportional representation to understand. This should make voters more confident and more willing to take part.

♦ **Fairness**
It is fairer to smaller parties than FPTP.

♦ **Broader representation**
Coalition governments may be produced by the use of this system so a broader spectrum of opinion will be represented in government, e.g. if this system was used in UK elections, it could result in a Labour and Liberal Democrat coalition.

♦ **Candidate choice**
Parties exercise more control over choice of candidates. This helps them to ensure the overall quality of the prospective parliamentary candidates.

Arguments against the Party List System

♦ **Voter – representative link**
Voters have no say over candidates. They will vote for the party and this may mean that they are 'allocated' a representative. This means that there is no effective link between the voters and their representative.

♦ **Under-representation**
The Party List System does not help under-represented groups to improve their representation, e.g. when placing people onto the list, the party may select people with a similar background to themselves. This may make it more difficult for working class, ethnic minorities and female candidates to make it onto the list.

♦ **Weakness of coalition governments**
Some people worry that coalition governments will be weak. They believe that the partners will not be able to agree on policy and will spend time arguing over detail, rather than running the country.

◆ Rise of extremist parties

As voters are voting for a party, it may be possible for a number of extremist parties to gain representatives. This may raise the profile and support of the party in the country as a whole, e.g. the British National Party may be able to get enough support for one or two representatives when all their support is calculated.

The Single Tranferable Vote (STV)

How does it work?

The country is divided into a number of large multi-member constituencies from which a number of candidates will be elected. In each constituency, as many as 4 MPs may be elected. Parties would put forward 4 candidates to be elected.

Voters cast their votes in order of preference, marking '1' against the name of the candidate they support most strongly, marking '2' against their second choice and '3' etc. against the names of the other candidates they support in order of preference. All of the votes are then counted and a formula is used to calculate which candidates have been successful.

To be elected, a candidate has to achieve a specific number of votes called a 'quota'. When a candidate achieves the quota of votes required, he or she is elected for that constituency. If he or she receives more votes than is required, the second preferences are redistributed to the other candidates. This continues until the right number of candidates has been elected.

Arguments for the Single Transferable Vote (STV)

◆ Improved representation

As each party will select a number of candidates for each constituency, it may encourage the selection of women and ethnic minority candidates. This will help to ensure a fairer balance in Parliament.

◆ Voter – representative link

STV maintains a strong link between voter and representative. Candidates are voted for directly unlike under many other PR systems like the Party List System.

◆ Coalition government

Coalition governments would usually be necessary under STV. This means that a broader spectrum of opinion will be represented in government. Policy solutions which a single party would not consider, may be adopted.

◆ Wasted votes

Fewer votes will be wasted as a number of candidates will be elected in each constituency. This means that a variety of parties may win some representation. In safe seats under FPTP, many voters may not participate because they believe that their vote will not make a difference.

◆ Greater choice

Voters can choose between candidates from the same party. This means that less effective candidates will not be guaranteed election. Under FPTP, in safe seats, the Conservative or Labour candidate will almost always win. Under STV, this might not always be the case.

Arguments against the Single Transferable Vote

◆ Complexity

STV is a complicated system for voters to understand. This may stop people from voting because they do not understand how candidates are to be elected. Only 58.2% voted in the 2001 election. If a new complicated system is introduced then the figures could fall even further.

◆ Confusion

As each constituency may elect four or more representatives, it may cause confusion. If a voter has a problem, it may be difficult to work out which representative to consult.

◆ Coalition government

Some people would argue that it might result in permanent coalition government. They would prefer to see one party with an overall majority providing strong government for the country.

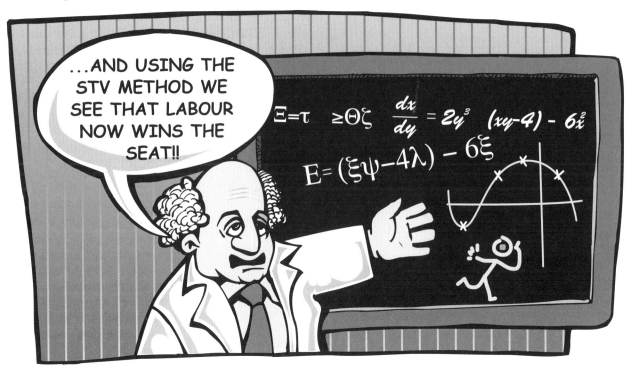

Results of the Scottish Parliament Elections 2003

Party	% Vote Constituency	% Vote Region	No. of seats Constituency	No. of seats Regional	No. of seats Total
Labour	35	30	46	4	50
SNP	24	22	9	18	27
Liberal Democrats	15	12	13	4	17
Conservatives	17	16	3	15	18
Scottish Socialists	6	6	0	6	6
Scottish Greens	0	6	0	7	7
Scottish Senior Citizens	0	2	0	1	1
Others	3	7	2	1	3

The Additional Member System (AMS)

AMS is a combination of FPTP and the Party List System. It is designed to include the advantages of both while avoiding the disadvantages. This system is used to elect MSPs to the Scottish Parliament.

How does it work?

As there are two aspects to this system, each voter has two votes to cast. One vote is used to elect a single constituency MSP and the other is used to express support for a party. The second votes are used to elect candidates from the party lists. This helps to make the overall result almost proportional.

Arguments for AMS

◆ **Proportionality**
AMS produces a fairly proportional result but still maintains a clear link between the voters and their representatives.

◆ **Coalition government**
Coalition government can be effective government that is willing to listen to different perspectives, e.g. the Labour/ Liberal Democrat coalition in the Scottish Parliament has introduced a number of policies that are dramatically different from the views of Labour controlled Westminster, including free personal care for the elderly and an end to tuition fees for Scottish university students.

◆ **Wasted votes**
Votes are not wasted under AMS. Even if a party has no chance of winning a constituency seat under the FPTP aspect, it can win party list seats as the Scottish Greens did in the 2003 election. This may encourage more voters to participate.

◆ **The two party system**
AMS allows a wider variety of views to be expressed. Under FPTP, the system is dominated by the two largest parties – Conservative and Labour. However, under AMS, smaller parties such as the Scottish Socialist Party and Greens have gained representation.

Arguments against AMS

◆ **Choice of candidates**
As the Party List aspect is used, many commentators would argue that too much power is given to the party in choosing candidates. This may mean that younger politicians will find it very difficult to be placed high enough up the list to have any real chance of being elected.

◆ **Conflict**
The system elects two types of representative. Some are directly elected for a constituency by the voters – constituency MSP. Others, very often from a different party, are elected by voters to cover a much larger area – list MSPs. This may cause ill feeling among MSPs of different parties.

◆ **Confusion**
The Scottish Parliament has both constituency and list MSPs. This may confuse voters who may be unsure whom to contact if a problem arises.

◆ **Extremist parties**
Some people are worried that extremist parties may have some representatives elected. This may provide them with a platform for their extremist views and allow them to secure even more support. The British National Party is a good example.

Health Care in the United Kingdom

(a)   The ways in which health care is provided and consumed. Patterns of health care and consumption. The degree to which there are social and geographical differences in health care provision and consumption. The degree to which socio-economic status and lifestyle affect and determine health care provision and consumption. Differences between state and private health care and consumption.

(b)   The extent to which health and patterns of health care are related to region, social class, gender, ethnic origin and age. Causes and consequences of patterns of health care provision and consumption. Case study of health care of the elderly (with reference to demographic trends, special needs, technological and other medical advances, community care).

(c)   The ways in which government and opposition policies influence the provision and consumption of health care. Differences in party policies and ideologies. The influence of differing interests and pressure groups within the field of health care.

Why is the National Health Service struggling to meet its original aims?

'From the cradle to the grave'

The National Health Service (NHS) was set up to look after the health of people in the UK 'from the cradle to the grave'. The NHS was to provide comprehensive, universal and free health care.

A comprehensive health service

The NHS was set up to provide comprehensive medical care for all. However, there are gaps in the services, with some patients being refused drugs because they are too expensive, for example Interferon B for Multiple Sclerosis sufferers. Many people who suffer from mental illness have also found it difficult to access the treatment they require. This has resulted in patients being placed in the community when they are not well enough to look after themselves. Frequently, they have to return to hospital for further treatment. This is known as 'the revolving door syndrome'.

A universal health service

The system is not universal, as there are inequalities in the delivery of health care in different parts of the country as a result of 'postcode prescribing' – treatments and/or medicinal drugs being available from the NHS in some parts of the UK but not available in others. The government has set up an audit of cancer care and treatment to discover the extent of postcode prescribing.

A free health service

The NHS was to provide health care free of charge at the point of delivery. However, many groups in the population would argue that this is no longer the case. Many patients have to pay towards the costs of dental care, prescriptions and eye tests. The government has also stated that elderly people should contribute towards the costs of their own personal care. Some pensioners have had to sell their family homes in order to meet their care costs.

Choice

Choice is another key principle underpinning the provision of health care in the UK. Patients have the freedom to choose whether to use the NHS or the private sector for their health care. However, the principle of choice does not exist throughout the service. NHS patients have little choice in choosing a surgeon, elderly people do not always get a choice of nursing home and poor people cannot afford treatment from the private sector.

The impact of devolution

At the outset, the UK government accepted that it should take responsibility for providing a centrally organised health care system for the people of Britain. This remains the situation today some fifty years on. However, with devolution, since 1999 the Scottish Parliament has had control over health care in Scotland while Westminster has retained responsibility for organising the health care system for England. This has meant that changes to the NHS like the introduction of 'foundation hospitals' will apply to England but not to Scotland.

Preventative medicine

The NHS has always believed that the prevention of disease should be just as important as the treatment of ill health. This is not only better for the health of the nation but also financially attractive to the NHS as it is much cheaper to prevent disease than to treat ill health. Through health education campaigns (eg, anti-smoking, healthy eating, exercise), immunisation programmes (eg, anti-flu and BCG, rubella in schools) and a certain amount of free health services (eg, free prescriptions for school children and sufferers from certain chronic illnesses), the NHS aims to encourage the prevention of illness. However, it is difficult to make a major impact in this area because many people are reluctant to take more responsibility for their own health or they may live in very poor conditions with little opportunity to escape.

Inequalities in Health

Evidence of gender inequalities in health

- 30% more boys than girls die in infancy
- Men are twice as likely to contract lung cancer
- 9 out of 10 people who live to more than 100 years of age are women
- The average man lives 5 years less than the average woman
- More boys than girls die during the first year of life
- There are on average 13 suicides a day in the UK, 9 are likely to be male and 4 are likely to be female
- Women are more likely to suffer from mental illness and depression than men
- 78% of prescriptions are issued to women

Causes of health inequalities between men and women

- Men are more likely to die earlier due to the number of risks that they take.
- Men are not as willing to go and see a doctor when something is wrong.
- Men are more likely to work in a physical manner and outside, putting them more at risk of disease and accident.

Solutions to health care problems for men and women

- There is a need for better education regarding the dangers from drugs, smoking and drinking.
- Both sexes need more information on the risks involved in drugs, smoking and drinking.
- Free counselling that is available to all when it is needed, dealing with issues such as PMT, post-natal depression, abortion and miscarriages for women and eating and cancer counselling for men.
- Screening for breast and cervical cancer for women and testicular and prostate cancer for men. (Screening for women has helped achieve government targets to reduce incidents and death rates from cancer. In 2001, there was a reduction in deaths among women aged 55-69 of 24.3%. The incidence of cervical cancer also fell by 30.9% between 1986 and 1998.)
- Well Man and Well Woman clinics to monitor the health of males and females. This will help to identify potential problems at an earlier stage, with a consequent better chance of full recovery.

Better education on diet, preventative measures, exercise and hygiene promotion.

Evidence of class inequalities in health

Males from the unskilled manual social class have a higher percentage reporting long standing illness than males from the professional social class. At age 65, only 49% of professional males report long standing illness while 66% of unskilled manual do.

Children from unskilled manual families are more likely never to visit the dentist or receive immunisation. 16% of children from professional classes never visit the dentist compared to 31% of unskilled manual. 6% of children from professional classes are not immunised against smallpox while 33% of unskilled manual are not immunised. A child from an unskilled social class is twice as likely to die before the age of 15 as a child who has a professional father.

Days of Restricted Activity as a Result of Poor Health

Males				Females			
0-15	16-44	45-64	65+	0-15	16-44	45-64	65+
Professional							
14	15	9	40	20	27	20	43
Employer & Manager							
15	13	18	31	10	22	24	48
Intermediate & junior non manual							
15	16	31	31	14	26	28	45
Skilled manual and own account non professional							
15	15	26	40	13	21	30	54
Semi-skilled manual							
24	12	29	49	9	25	42	65
Unskilled manual							
18	16	55	45	19	25	33	53

Note that class differences become greater as people grow older and differences exist for males and females.

Variations in Health, Behaviour and Status by Neighbourhood Type in Glasgow (%)

	Least deprived	Most deprived
Teenage mothers	3	17
Mothers who smoke	11	43
Mothers who breast feed	51	22
Babies with low birth weight	5	10
People eating low fat spread	16	8
People eating white bread	17	70
People who smoke	34	50
People with high alcohol consumption	21	39
People overweight	25	29
People being treated for heavy alcohol/drug use	4	18

Incidence of Chronic Illness by Social Class

Condition/group per 10,000 of population

	Professional, Employer and Manager	Intermediate and non manual	Skilled	Manual	Semi-skilled	Unskilled
Heart	67	90	77	95	117	134
Respiratory	56	58	64	71	80	102
Digestive	30	34	32	42	53	70
Musculoskeletal	98	132	141	163	187	235

Causes of health inequalities amongst the social classes

- ◆ Evidence shows that the professional classes take fuller advantage of the services provided by the NHS compared to uptake by the unskilled manual classes.
- ◆ The unskilled manual classes may also face increased health problems because charges for dental care and prescriptions act as a deterrent to accessing health care.
- ◆ The working classes are more likely to live in poorer housing conditions resulting in a number of long term illnesses.
- ◆ Poor diet due to an inability to buy healthy foodstuffs, e.g. vegetables in their own area.
- ◆ Poor uptake of preventative health services.
- ◆ A lower level of education may mean that they do not understand how important it is to look after their own and their family's health.
- ◆ Middle classes are more likely to participate in health promoting activities such as exercise and healthy diet.
- ◆ Babies from lower socio-economic classes are more likely to be born to mothers suffering from poor health.
- ◆ Children from lower socio-economic classes are more likely to have a poorer diet, less stimulation and fewer safe play areas.

Case Study

Scotland cuts cancer rates

Scotland has recorded a fall in the number of cancer cases recorded. The success of campaigns aimed at encouraging Scots to give up smoking is the main reason for this. Scotland still has the highest rates of cancer but these are falling while those for England and Wales are both increasing.

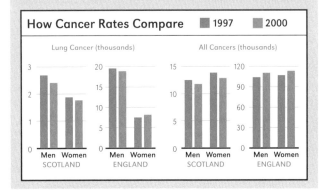

Solutions

Tackling poverty
If everyone who wants to work has a job, they should be more able to look after themselves. This will involve investment in the most disadvantaged neighbourhoods, as poverty is one of the main causes of health inequalities. Men in professional occupations have similar rates of death wherever they live but rates vary greatly amongst the different classes.

Health education programmes
Health education programmes and a cut in advertising would help to reduce consumption of alcohol and cut smoking. A ban on advertising at sporting events, as demanded by the European Union, is already in place.

Responsibility
Try to encourage individuals to take more responsibility for their own health.

Preventative medicine
A greater emphasis on preventative medicine, especially in poorer sections of society.

Housing
Government to take charge of housing policy to ensure that every individual has access to decent housing.

Life skills
Develop a programme to encourage life skills which will help all citizens to take an active part in their own health.

Life expectancy
The government has set a target to reduce the gap between the health authorities with the lowest life expectancy at birth and the population as a whole by a minimum of 10 per cent. At present for men, the local authority with the highest life expectancy at birth was East Dorset with 79.0 years while in Glasgow it is only 68.7 years.

Life Expectancy in Britain (years)		
Year	Woman	Men
1920	55.0	51.0
1930	63.0	58.0
1950	71.0	66.0
1970	75.0	69.0
1990	79.0	73.0
2000	79.6	74.4

Evidence of race inequalities in health

Ethnic minorities suffer from a higher ratio of liver cancer, diabetes, hypertension and strokes.

Causes
First generation immigrants may be more prone to certain diseases due to the climate and conditions in their country of origin.
Language problems may mean that some immigrants have difficulty in explaining the nature of their health problems to the doctor, resulting in patients being given inappropriate treatment.

Solutions

♦ Encourage and train more health service professionals from ethnic minority backgrounds in order to help overcome some of the language problems.

♦ Need to educate the ethnic minority communities about health issues and make it easier for them to access the health care professional.

Private Health Care

Arguments in Favour

♦ A partnership between the NHS and the private sector may help to cut some waiting lists. Some health authorities are already sending heart patients to private hospitals for operations.

♦ If private hospitals and staff are used to provide health care, then it may be possible to cut the cost of providing health care in the UK. This would make the government popular because they could either cut taxation or use the extra money to finance other services such as education and transport.

♦ If the NHS joins with the private sector, the total amount of money available for health care in the UK will increase. This may mean that more money can be put into research and development or used to help purchase new technology which can help to save lives.

♦ By developing the NHS and the private sector, patients will be given a choice. This should result in competition and improvements in the quality of the services that are provided. People will be able to pick the best quality of care and this will encourage the weaker parts to improve.

Arguments Against

♦ Many people think that there should only be one health care provider in the UK– the NHS. This service should be available to all citizens of the UK and be free at the point of delivery but paid for through taxation. This will help to ensure that health care is the same for all and that money should not influence access to health care.

♦ When private hospitals have a medical emergency that cannot be dealt with, they rely on the NHS to provide the care that is required. If NHS doctors are looking after a private patient, they may not be available to provide care for an NHS patient.

♦ There are lengthy waiting lists in the UK. This may be partially due to the number of doctors and nurses working in the private sector, providing, for example, cosmetic surgery. Their skills would be better used saving lives.

♦ Very few people can pay the large insurance premiums that are needed to access private sector health care. This will result in a two-tier service in which NHS patients have to wait for health care while private patients are able to jump the queue.

Involving the Private Sector in the NHS

The Private Finance Initiative (PFI)

PFI is the Private Finance Initiative that was set up by the Conservatives when in government. PPP which stands for Public Private Partnership Programmes was the new name given by Labour to PFI when they came to power in 1997.

Arguments in favour

- If the private sector and the public sector can join together to help improve health care in the UK then it must be worth pursuing. If each side can learn from the strengths of the other, then the quality of health care will get better. If this opportunity is missed then it will make improvement much more difficult. Waiting lists may get longer and costs may go up.
- Working with the private sector to provide hospitals will help to spread taxpayers' money further and may increase the number of hospitals and help to cut waiting lists and the time spent on these lists. If all plans go ahead, the country should have an extra 15 hospitals by 2004.
- Under normal circumstances, it takes 10 years to build a hospital under the control of the public sector. The use of PPP will help to reduce the timescale from 10 to about 4 years.
- More beds will help to improve the services that people receive and help to save the lives of patients who require emergency care.
- Services in hospitals provided by PPP finance will also improve, with greater emphasis placed on 'hotel type' services such as telephones, catering, internet and television. If this helps to relax patients, then we may find that patients get better more quickly and this will save the NHS money. This money could be used to provide more doctors and nurses.

Arguments against

- PFI/PPP will cost the taxpayer more in the long run. The BMA claims that the Edinburgh Royal Infirmary will cost the government £270 million over 25 years. If they had used the normal form of finance, the figure would be closer to £180m.
- PFI/PPP hospitals are designed in part by the private sector. They will be more interested in keeping costs down and not concerned about patient care. If profit is more important than patient care, patients may end up being treated in sub-standard conditions.
- Many people think that PPP is nothing more than privatisation of the NHS through the back door. They argue that once PPP companies become involved, the original principles behind the NHS will be lost forever, and those people in society who cannot provide for themselves will suffer.
- PPP hospitals may encourage their use for treatment of private patients. As there will already be fewer beds in the hospitals, waiting lists for NHS patients will actually increase and the gap in health care will widen.

What are the implications of the growth in the elderly population?

Some elderly people find that their health worsens as they get older. They may face chronic illness and mobility problems. This may mean that they lose their independence and rely on families for help. They also may face osteoarthritis; rheumatoid arthritis; cardiovascular disease; hypertension; strokes; dementia; Alzheimer's disease; diabetes; loss of hearing; tinnitus; incontinence; osteoporosis; blindness.

Older people demand more from the NHS. Over 75 year olds make the greatest demands, e.g., in 1991 the NHS spent an average of just over £500 per person. However, the average expenditure was £250 for people between 5-64 and £2,200 for people over 75.

The number of taxpayers is falling at the same time as the number of elderly people is increasing. This means that it is going to be more difficult for the state to provide for the needs of all elderly people. Taxes will have to increase or the money will have to be taken away from other government services. Both of these solutions may make any future government unpopular. This is called the 'demographic timebomb'.

Older people are heavier consumers of prescriptions than the rest of the population. Just over half (52.3%) of all prescriptions in England go to pensioners.

Case Study – Health Care of the Elderly

To what extent do the elderly all make the same demands on the NHS?

Every person is different and some people age faster than others. Some people in their 60s may look and act much older than some people in their 80s.

Some people can afford to use private health care and therefore make little demand on NHS services. However, most elderly people do make use of the NHS. Only 3% of over 75s have a healthcare plan.

Some elderly people make use of day care services and receive help at home. Others rely on family and friends.

In England, in 2000, there were 208,000 residential care places for over 65s while most others were still able to have some level of independence. Residential care can be used to provide long term care; respite care; recovery from operations; hospice care.

Elderly people who live in good quality housing are more likely to avoid some illnesses. However, there is a higher percentage of elderly people living in poor housing than any other group.

On average, men over 65 make six visits each year to their GP, compared to three for men between 16 and 44. Women over 65 make six visits to the GP, compared to five for women between 16 and 44.

Those aged over 75 are more likely to visit their GP or have an outpatient visit than younger adults.

5% of those over 65 and about 20% of those over 85 need long-term care.

Case Study – Bed Blocking

Bed blocking is the name given to a situation where an elderly patient cannot be discharged from hospital because of a lack of community care provision. This results in hospital beds being denied to other patients in need.

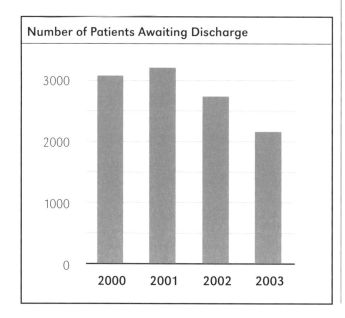

Number of Patients Awaiting Discharge

- In October 2003, 2210 elderly patients were awaiting to be discharged.
- 94 patients were stuck in Scottish hospitals for more than a year.
- £30m is spent per year to solve the bed blocking problem.
- Delays in being assessed for a care package is the main reason for 500 patients who are well enough to leave hospital but too vulnerable to return to their homes taking up hospital places.
- 438 patients were waiting for an available nursing home place.
- 310 patients were waiting for funding towards a care home place.
- Scottish Executive has created 'rapid response teams' to provide care packages for people in their own home ensuring that 1000 patients per month are being discharged earlier from hospital.

Changes in the number of elderly people in the United Kingdom

◆ The population of the UK has grown steadily. However, the elderly population has increased as a proportion of the total population.

◆ The proportion of people in the 75+ age group is projected to increase from 4% in 1961 to 9% in 2021.

◆ An increased number of over 75s could have a significant impact on the provision of health services and community care.

◆ Life expectancy in the UK in 2003 was 78.2. In Japan, it was 80.9; in France, 79.3; in Germany, 78.4, in USA 77.1.

◆ Life expectancy in 1998 was 74 years for men and 79.8 years for women. In 1931, it was 58.1 for men and 62.1 for women.

◆ As more people become aware of the importance of living a healthy lifestyle, and modern medicine and technology continue to improve, life expectancy is expected to increase. The elderly population is therefore getting larger. In 1999, there were 9.3 million people over 65 in the UK but by the year 2026 this figure will increase to 13.2 million.

The results of technological change and medical advances

◆ Many elderly people have improved health and housing conditions. This means that many people live longer and have a better quality of life.

◆ Medical technology has helped many elderly people to live longer and have a better quality of life. New techniques have been developed in heart surgery, cataract operations and replacement hips and joints.

◆ Technology also allows some elderly people to live longer in their own homes. Aids and adaptations include chair lifts; medical alarms; observation cameras; tracking bracelets.

◆ Research into new drugs has allowed many elderly people to overcome a number of diseases that, in the past, would have changed or ended their life. Examples include drugs to thin the blood or to protect against ulcers.

◆ The NHS may be a victim of its own success. More elderly people are surviving to well past retirement age. This may cause a demographic time bomb as fewer workers have to pay more tax to ensure that elderly people receive the care that they deserve.

◆ As technology improves, some people may expect the NHS to solve all health problems. Since this is not possible, some people will always see the NHS as a failure.

Government help for the elderly

The government has taken action to improve health care for the elderly. In July 2000, the NHS plus proposed a number of changes including: action to tackle waiting times; £10m to improve cleanliness; an extra 20,000 nurses; modern matrons

to take responsibility for the standard of care. However, some elderly people are still concerned about: long delays for older patients waiting for admission from Accident and Emergency (A&E); low levels of skills to meet the particular needs of elderly patients; negative attitudes towards older people; decisions made without the full involvement of elderly people.

Improvements required include: a need to respect the privacy and dignity of patients by changing the attitudes of staff; better community services and discharge arrangements for elderly people to help them to receive care in the most appropriate setting.

The Scottish Executive has promised to provide central heating for every elderly person by 2005.

In 1998, the government set up the Royal Commission on Long-Term Care. It stated that personal care should be free to the user and paid for through taxation. The user should only be charged board and lodging costs. The UK Government rejected this for England but the Scottish Parliament put it into operation from April 2002.

Arguments for Community Care

◆ Historically, there were many cases of poor standards of care. Some individuals who were looked after in old institutions generally had a poor quality of life, in which there was little freedom or choice. If they are looked after in the community they have more responsibility to make decisions about their own future. They can decide what to eat, when to eat, when to sleep etc.

◆ With an increase in the number of elderly people, it is very expensive to have institutional care. Taxpayers would have to put more money into this type of care. This would either mean an increase in taxation or a cut in other services. It is expected that Community Care will save the taxpayer money by transferring some of the burden from the state to the family.

◆ Many studies show that people will have a better quality of life if they are looked after in familiar surroundings. Their stress levels will be lower and they will have people to talk to. Consequently, costs to the state fall.

◆ In the past, no single agency had the responsibility for the care of individuals. Sometimes, a social worker, a hospital nurse and a doctor may all have played a part in the care of an elderly person. However, if something went wrong it was very difficult to work out which part of the system was at fault. With Community Care, social workers now have overall responsibility. This should help to improve the quality of care that patients receive.

◆ As drug technology and availability has developed, more health problems can be dealt with in the community by patients themselves. This saves the taxpayer money.

◆ Community Care was designed to support the six million carers in the UK. Carers are people who look after friends or relatives in the community but get little in the way of support from the government. Community Care should help to ensure that they receive some financial support and also short breaks from having to care. Elderly people would receive respite care, i.e., would stay in a nursing home for a few days.

Arguments against Community Care

- Many elderly people who are discharged from hospital into the community are not able to survive, especially in the long term. This may be because they have lived in an institution for too long or because they stop taking (or forget to take) the drugs that they need.
- Teams of doctors and nurses who work in institutions build up an understanding of an individual's problems over a number of years. They are able to identify exactly what the patient needs. When the teams are split up under Community Care, much of this expertise may be lost, as social workers may not always have the range of skills needed.
- Community Care was designed to save the taxpayer money. However, many local authorities are finding that they don't have enough money to ensure that all patients are looked after with dignity. In Surrey, the local authority ran out of money and had to ask private nursing homes to look after patients for free.
- Care is provided according to the money available. Care should be provided for all who need it, irrespective of cost.
- Many people are 'slipping through the net' and left to look after themselves until a bed is available.
- Some elderly people are known as 'revolving door' patients because they are always in and out of care.

Recent health care reforms

- The Welsh Assembly has decided to make eye tests free. If this cuts the number of serious eye diseases in the Welsh population it may encourage other parts of the country to follow. The Scottish Parliament is going to pay for personal medical and nursing care costs for the elderly. This is following a recommendation of the Royal Commission. The elderly in other parts of the UK may start to demand the same level of treatment.
  The Prime Minister, Tony Blair, thinks that the better-off elderly people should pay their own costs.
- More is spent on health care in Scotland than the rest of the UK. This was originally provided to help with some of the bigger health problems that existed in Scotland. Spending per year on health is: £1041 in England; £1271 in Scotland; £1180 in Wales; £1193 in Northern Ireland.
- The UK government is planning to encourage greater use of private medicine. This could include more partnerships between NHS and private hospitals. NHS patients could also be sent to private hospitals for operations.
- The Labour government has promised to increase the funding of health care in the UK. They will also introduce 20,000 more nurses, 7,500 consultants and 2000 GPs.
- GP Fundholding was ended and the Internal Market was ended. The government wanted to end competition and instead get the different agencies to work together. These groups would be called Primary Care Groups. These groups would provide the care for an area and this would be monitored by the Local Health Authority. Primary Care Groups aimed to: improve the quality of care and offer better integration of services; improve health and address health inequalities; commission hospital services for their patients.

- In 1997, the Labour Manifesto stated that they would cut waiting lists. However, as there are still more than 1 million on the lists many would argue that they have failed. Others would argue that the number on the list may be coming down but the time spent on the list by patients is increasing. The First Minister, Jack McConnell, has said that he wants to end waiting list targets and concentrate more on waiting times.
- To attract more professionals, the government increased pay. Newly qualified nurses were given a 12% pay rise and other grades received more than 4%.
- More than 100 new hospital developments have been given the go-ahead between 2000 and 2010. Many will be paid from Public Private Partnerships (PPP).
- Other changes include: providing better hospital food; better bedside facilities including televisions and telephones; encouraging more patient involvement; working with the private sector through the Private Finance Initiative (PFI) and PPP; NHS Direct – a telephone helpline to give patients immediate healthcare advice; NHS Direct On-line (help on the internet).
- The UK spent 6.8% of Gross Domestic Product (GDP) on health in 2002. This is more than £1 billion every day but still below the European Union (EU) average of 8.6%.
- Some people argue that more money will not solve all the problems. Waiting lists in Scotland have spiralled since 1999, with more than 11023 people added to the national total; outpatients are waiting longer for appointments, the average up by 10 days to 57; diseases such as lung cancer still claim a huge number of lives; mortality rates from cancer and heart disease are higher in Scotland than anywhere else in the UK.
- In the 2002 Budget, Chancellor Gordon Brown promised to increase health spending in the UK in line with other developed economies. He will increase spending from £65.4 billion in 2002 to £105.6 billion in 2007. This represents an increase of 43 per cent after inflation. This means an increase from 6.7% of GDP in 1997 to 9.4% in 2007.

Arguments for the Patients' Charter

- The Patients' Charter highlighted the rights and responsibilities of each patient. If more people are aware of their rights it may help to improve the quality of the service for two reasons: firstly, hospital staff are more likely to provide the publicised service and, secondly, because patients may complain if the quality of the service received is not up to standard to which they are entitled.
- One of the rights relates to time on waiting lists. Patients should be entered on to a waiting list when a GP refers them to the hospital. The maximum time on the list has been cut from 2 years to 18 months. This may help to cut the time that patients have to wait.
- The Patients' Charter will encourage all people involved in health care to take part in the evaluation of the service. If people didn't ask questions about the quality of the service, managers would find it more difficult to highlight problems and suggest solutions.
- The Patients' Charter will make all NHS staff accountable for their actions. This should encourage underachieving staff to improve the quality of their work. If they don't, then patient complaints may lead to disciplinary action.

Arguments against the Patients' Charter

- Most people have little idea of what the Patients' Charter contains. Indeed, many people may not be aware of its existence. Most of those who are not aware of their rights will never complain and this may result in a health gap.
- The document does outline rights and responsibilities. However, these rights are not backed by the law.
- In many cases, when patients complain, little or nothing is done about it.
- The number of patient complaints has increased and managers are having to spend more time dealing with problems. However, this may mean that they are able to spend less time dealing with the day-to-day management of hospitals and care may therefore decline.
- Some people think that the Charter is nothing more than a paper exercise.

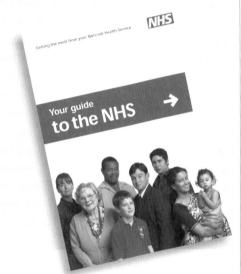

Arguments for health promotion schemes

- Health promotion is about preventing illness rather than trying to cure the person after they have become ill.
- The government has spent a great deal of money on education campaigns. The 'Be all you can be' campaign and the Health Education Board's (HEB's) broadcast by Gavin Hastings are two good examples of how the government tries to use the media to educate the people.
- The Scottish Executive has also placed a great deal of importance on screening programmes for men and women. It is now common for women to get a cervical smear every three years. More needs to be done to encourage men to participate in schemes to prevent testicular and prostate cancer.
- Health centres and GP practices are given financial incentives to encourage patients to take part in prevention schemes. If a certain percentage sign up to a scheme, then the centres and practices receive a financial bonus at the end of the year.
- The Scottish Executive is trying to encourage healthy lifestyles by setting doctors, hospitals and Primary Health Groups targets in terms of immunisations.

Arguments against health promotion schemes

- The government can encourage people to follow a healthy lifestyle but individuals must take responsibility for their own health. Many people know what is required but don't always follow advice. The government needs to encourage individuals to make lifestyle changes.
- Preventative measures can't stop all diseases. It may help to stop cancers spreading but cancer is still one of the biggest killers.
- GPs find it very difficult to make any real progress with certain groups in society. The wealthy and the middle class are more likely to follow advice given. Poorer sections of society and the socially excluded have made little in the way of progress. The government needs to target resources at these groups.
- One of the biggest causes of poor health in the UK is smoking but the government has so far refused to ban smoking advertising at sporting events. If people associate smoking with sport, more may take up the habit. If the government is serious about promoting healthy lifestyles, then it must take responsibility for the damage that this may be doing.

Politics of Food

In relation to Africa (excluding South Africa).

(a) Reasons for food shortage: the problems of exploiting and distributing resources; political economic and social inequalities; land tenure and use; development policies; the impact of war.

(b) Response to food shortages: changes in international aid; agricultural policies and famine relief; role of non-governmental organisations (NGOs); British Government policies on overseas food aid; effectiveness of these responses.

(c) How power is exercised, internally and externally, in the control and supply of food by governments and relief agencies.

Causes of Food Shortages in Africa

There are many causes of food shortages in Africa. Usually a combination of war, debt, dependence on cash crop production, population growth, land ownership, political problems and the climate means that large groups of people do not have access to enough food to ensure that a healthy standard of living can be maintained.

War

War makes it difficult to produce food and to transport it to those who are most in need. In countries such as the Sudan, people find it difficult to meet their need for food because of civil war. The North of Sudan is controlled by an Islamic government which wants the whole country to follow Muslim laws. However, the South of Sudan is controlled by Christians who do not wish to follow the laws of a religion that they do not believe in. Since the 1970s, more than one million people have been killed in this civil war between the Muslim North and the Christian South.

War causes food shortages because the government spends money on weapons with little kept aside to meet the needs of the people. In the Sudan, little is spent on education or health. This means that conditions in the country are unlikely to improve and many people die from preventable diseases. Many people are frightened by the war and think it would be much safer to leave the country and become refugees in neighbouring countries like Ethiopia and Chad. However, when people are forced to leave the land, they have no means of supporting themselves and have to live in camps where food is provided for them.

Sometimes there is simply not enough food to feed all of the people in the refugee camps. When people leave the land, there is no one to look after the crops and they die. This means that there is less food for sale in the markets and more people will face food shortages.

Debt

In the 1970s, many African countries were encouraged to take out loans from rich banks in the North – Europe and North America. However, this money was not always used to meet the needs of the people. When interest rates increased, countries had to pay back even more which obviously resulted in a fall in expenditure on areas like education, health care and transport. The United Nations estimates that 19,000 children now die each day in the developing world because of debt. Some countries are concerned that they may never be able to pay back their loans. For every £1 that countries like the Sudan have borrowed, they have to pay back £13

OK POOR NATIONS – BEFORE WE ALLOW YOU TO BORROW MORE MONEY, THIS IS WHAT YOU MUST DO...

...COMBINED WITH CURRENCY REALIGNMENT AND AGRICULTURAL CONSOLIDATION.

WHAT DOES HE MEAN?

...AN APPROPRIATE REDUCTION IN DEPARTMENTAL BUDGETARY PROJECTIONS...

EAT LESS!

because of interest and default payments. Debt causes food shortages because governments cannot afford to buy supplies for their people or ensure that more food is made available. Improvements such as better education or health care, better irrigation schemes or improved transport networks simply cannot be afforded.

Countries end up using any spare money to pay back debt. In some cases, countries have to use 20% of national income to pay back debt. It is estimated that Sudan's debt is in excess of £15 billion. The 52 poorest countries now owe the rich hundreds of billions in unpayable debts and are spending more on debt than on health and education combined. Some countries are trying to cancel debt but many groups, such as Jubilee 2000, would argue that this is not happening quickly enough.

Cash crop production

Many governments encourage the growth of cash crops which can be sold to other countries (coffee, tea, sugar) rather than growing food to feed their own people. In the Sudan, people were encouraged to grow cotton and sugar and sell it to the rich countries of the world. The price that African farmers receive for their crops is usually well below what would be a fair price. For example, the price of coffee has not increased for 50 years. This makes it difficult for African farmers to earn enough money to buy food to feed their families. Farmers usually only have a small piece of land to grow cash crops which makes it difficult to meet their family's needs and often results in under employment (not enough work for all the family members). In Tanzania, farmers may receive £7 a month for the coffee they produce. However, this will only be enough to feed their families for two days. This leaves them having to face the question of where they find the money to feed their families for the rest of the month.

Population growth

The population of many African countries is growing for a number of reasons.

- Many people do not understand or have access to family planning.
- Health care has improved so people are living longer.
- Traditionally families are larger than in other parts of the world - this is because people want children who can look after them when they are older.

As the population in Africa increases, food shortages will increase because there are more mouths to feed. Sudan has a population of about 30,000,000 with an annual growth rate of 2.4%. This compares to an annual growth rate in the UK population of 0.1%.

Land ownership

In Africa, land ownership by individuals does not exist to the same extent that it exists in other parts of the world. In the past, land was owned by the tribe and used by individual farmers. However, after colonisation, that changed and in many countries the rich took control of the most productive land. Sudan is a large country but the best use is not made of the land that is available. Only a small percentage of the available farmland is used for cultivation. Also, the government broke up the tribal system of land ownership and took all land that was not formally registered into state ownership. This meant that many farmers no longer had access to land which could be used to grow crops. The government of Sudan has also allowed Saudi Arabia to use Sudanese land for their own crop production. This again reduces the amount of land available for crop production by the people of Sudan.

Political problems

For many reasons, governments in Africa have failed to make best use of the raw materials that they have available. Countries like the Sudan do face difficulties but the actions of the government have not helped.

- In the Sudan, the civil war uses up most of the resources of the government. This means that there is little left to make improvements in education, health care or transport. This would suggest that there is little prospect of improvement in the long run.
- There is also a lot of arable land that is not used in the Sudan. If they were to invest in the land they had available, to meet the needs of the people, fewer people would die from starvation. Investing in new technology would make a big difference.
- The government of the Sudan was also slow to admit that they had a famine in 1998. This meant that aid was slow to arrive and many people who died could have been helped.

The climate

Many countries are faced with environmental problems. In the Sudan in 1984, the rainfall was the lowest ever recorded. A lack of rain caused the crops to fail and the deserts to spread, resulting in a reduction in the available land for growing crops. Some countries are also faced with flash floods like the ones that hit Mozambique in the late 1990s. All the crops were destroyed and the people were infected with various diseases which were spread by the water.

WFP/Kenya/B Barton

Response to Food Shortages

Bilateral aid

Bilateral aid is aid provided directly by one country to another country that may be in need, e.g. the UK government may send aid to help people in the Sudan. More than half of all aid provided by the UK is bilateral aid. This gives the donor country a great deal of control over the destination of the aid.

What are the advantages of bilateral aid?

✓ Sometimes, bilateral aid, because it is sent directly from one country to another, can get to those people who are in need more quickly. This means that lives can be saved that would be lost under other forms of aid.

The British government has rejected former methods of providing bilateral aid such as Aid for Trade on the grounds that the aid was being used to benefit businesses rather than ordinary people. In 2001, the Department for International Development called on all countries to ensure that aid was used to promote the development of the poorest groups.

✓ Bilateral aid can be targeted at governments that will make effective use of the help. In May 2002, US president George Bush promised to increase aid by $5 billion to countries with sound economic policies. This will help to ensure that aid is not wasted.

What are the disadvantages of bilateral aid?

✗ Bilateral aid is often tied aid. This means that a country, like the Sudan, is given aid but must spend the money on goods from the donor country. This may mean that the countries receiving the aid sometimes have to pay more for the goods they purchase and they often cannot buy the goods that they really want. This may mean that the aid is not as effective as it could be. 60% of all bilateral aid is tied aid.

✗ Sometimes the aid that is given will come in the form of a loan. This may help a country to buy goods and services but it may also mean that the country ends up in debt because it cannot pay back the loan and interest.

✗ Aid does not always get to the people who need it most. The Sudan is a large country and often the aid only reaches the large cities and ports. This means that many people in rural areas do not receive any help.

✗ Sometimes the government does not use the aid to help the people who are most in need. In the Sudan, there is a fear that aid is being used to buy weapons to sustain the civil war, rather than help the people in the poorest parts of the country.

✗ Bilateral aid projects are usually agreed between governments, usually involving large-scale projects, like the building of airports. However, this will not be of direct help to individuals who are failing to meet their basic needs.

✗ Some people in the UK would argue that 'our' money should be spent on 'our' people. They would ask why taxpayers' money should be wasted in this way. Are there not people in the UK who require help?

✗ Bilateral aid does not always reach those who are in greatest need. The American government is often criticised for giving aid to countries or groups that have similar political or religious views as themselves. Similarly, the former Communist countries like the USSR were more likely to give aid to Ethiopia which also had a Communist government..

✗ Many countries do not invest enough of their wealth in bilateral aid to make it effective. The UN target for aid is 0.7% of each country's national wealth but many countries fall short of this target. Only five countries currently meet the target - Denmark, Norway, Luxembourg, the Netherlands and Sweden. The UK government has started to reverse the recent decline but still falls short of the target, spending 0.33% of wealth on aid. This shortfall may mean that aid fails to meet the needs of all the affected people.

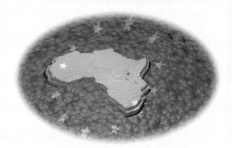

Multilateral aid

Multilateral aid is aid which is provided through international agencies or organisations like the European Union or agencies of the United Nations like WHO, FAO or UNICEF. Many governments provide the funds needed by these international organisations.

How successful is multilateral aid?

✓ Multilateral agencies usually have large amounts of money that they can use to fund projects in different parts of the world. UNICEF, for example, works in more than 140 countries around the world.

✓ More than 2,000,000 people in the Sudan have benefited from emergency supplies sent by UNICEF.

✓ Most of the UK aid budget is spent by multilateral agencies like the EU. This means that, together, the different countries can have enough money to make a difference.

✓ Multilateral agencies can afford to be involved in long-term projects. This means that they can see large-scale projects through from start to finish and ensure that the aid is being efficiently used.

✓ Through the specialised agencies of the UN, it can almost be guaranteed that aid will get to those people who need it most. UNICEF collected money in 2002 through the 'UNICEF day for change' project. This money was then used to help children get a proper education.

✓ The World Food Programme, which is part of the United Nations, managed to persuade the Sudanese government in November 2001 to agree to a four day cease fire to enable them to distribute food in Southern Sudan. The Khartoum government had previously blockaded all humanitarian aid since 1989.

What are the arguments against multilateral aid?

✗ Some people argue that multilateral agencies are slow to react in time of crisis. With the emergency in the Sudan in 1998, the agencies were slow to react and many people may have lost their lives as a direct result.

✗ Much of the aid may not be getting through to the poorest groups. When agencies work with governments, much of the aid is used to support urban projects. This does not help those in rural areas who often have bigger problems to deal with.

✗ Agencies like UNESCO do not take sufficient account of the views of local people. If agencies were to involve local people more in decision-making, aid could be targeted at the areas of greatest need and in a way that would ensure the greatest long-term benefits.

✗ Sometimes the aid that is provided by agencies is so slow to arrive that, when eventually food arrives in the areas of greatest need, it just causes other problems. Sometimes aid from the EU has arrived just when farmers have grown their first new harvest. This means that people will not pay the farmers for their food and therefore the farmers may face hunger as a result.

✗ Some people criticise EU aid as being nothing more than a cheap method of disposing of food that has been collected because of the failure of the Common Agricultural Policy. Often the food is not what the people in the receiving country are used to.

WFP by CMB/Antwerp

Sudan CASE STUDY

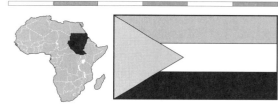

Sudan is geographically Africa's largest country and is one of the poorest countries on earth. One quarter of the population will not live past the age of 40 years. About 64% of the female population and 32% of the male population are illiterate and more than one third of five year olds are under weight. Sudan has suffered from war for 34 out of the last 45 years.

The long-running civil war between the Arab Muslims of the North and the Black African Christians of the South has caused major problems. Some people think that more than two million people have been killed by war and famine in the last 15 years and five million have been displaced as refugees.

Multilateral agencies are often a target for both sides in the civil war. At a World Food Programme feeding station in the South, where more than 4,000 people were queuing for food, helicopter gunships were used to fire on unarmed civilians. Actions like this will make starving people stay away, even though they are obviously in need of help.

Basic Indicators

Total population (000s)	31,095
Gross national income per capita	320 US$

Mortality

Infant mortality rate (per 1,000 live births)	66
Under 5 mortality rate (per 1,000 live births)	108
Life expectancy	55.6

Water and Sanitation

% population with access to safe water	
Urban	86
Rural	69
% population with access to adequate sanitation	
Urban	87
Rural	48

Nutrition

% under 5 suffering moderate and severe malnutrition	34

Education

Education	Male	Female
Adult literacy rate	68	46
Primary school enrolment ratio	48	48
Secondary school enrolment ratio	21	19

Popperfoto/Reuter

Angola CASE STUDY

After years of civil war in Angola between the warring factions, FAA and UNITA, a peace agreement was signed in April 2002. This allowed humanitarian agencies for the first time to assess fully the scale of the country's problems. About 50% of the population were found to suffer from acute malnutrition and 25% to be in need of urgent medical assistance. Angola has the second highest infant mortality rate in the world.

Angola has the largest percentage of internally displaced persons with a total of 4 million people displaced as a result of years of civil war. It is estimated that 100,000 children have been separated from their parents by the war and that as many as 700,000 children have lost at least one parent.

Most deaths of children aged under 5 are attributable to preventable diseases. Although vaccination rates for diseases like measles remain low, malaria is the largest single cause of childhood mortality.

Malnutrition has reached 30% amongst children. By September 2002, the World Food Programme was feeding 1.2 million people, with this figure expected to increase to 1.9 million by December 2002. The government, in partnership with humanitarian agencies like UNICEF, is leading efforts to reduce malnutrition rates. High protein biscuits have been distributed to supplementary feeding centres throughout Angola to improve the health and nutrition of moderately malnourished adults and children.

In spite of ongoing efforts to improve access to safe water, provision varies greatly across Angola between urban and rural areas. 46% of the urban population have access to improved water supplies but only 20% of the rural population.

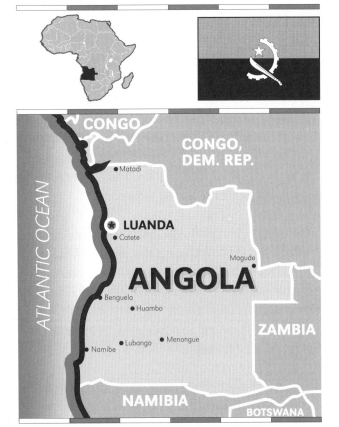

The education system has low enrolment levels with only 50% of children of school age receiving a formal education. It is estimated that 1 million children remain outwith primary education.

Basic Indicators	
Total population (000s)	13,134
Gross national income per capita	240 US$

Mortality	
Infant mortality rate (per 1,000 live births)	172
Under 5 mortality rate (per 1,000 live births)	295
Life expectancy	40.1

Water and Sanitation	
% population with access to safe water	
Urban	34
Rural	40
% population with access to adequate sanitation	
Urban	70
Rural	30

Nutrition	
% under 5 suffering moderate and severe malnutrition	42

Education	Male	Female
Adult literacy rate	n/a	54
Primary school enrolment ratio	95	95
Secondary school enrolment ratio	n/a	n/a

Non Governmental Organisations (NGOs)

What are the arguments for NGOs providing aid to the people of Africa?

Non Governmental Organisations such as Save the Children, Oxfam and Christian Aid are often more successful than governments in providing aid. This is because NGOs tend to focus on small scale projects which aim to help those in the greatest need. For example, Christian Aid has been helping 4,000 households in the Ethiopian Rift Valley to improve the soil and grow the food that they need to survive.

NGOs can often work as pressure groups and are able to influence government decision-makers, both in donor countries and in the developing world. Oxfam and other groups work together as part of the Jubilee 2000 Campaign to push for debt relief for the poorest countries in the world. This may have helped to cut Tanzania's debt by $3 billion.

NGOs also help to focus the aid given by governments, businesses and individuals towards those in greatest need. Governments now understand that these organisations have a greater knowledge of where the problems are and can ensure that the aid gets to the areas of greatest need.

There are millions of people who have been helped by aid that is directed by NGOs. In 2002, Save the Children set up projects to help with the food crisis in Malawi. A poor harvest, widespread flooding and a massive increase in the price of food left millions of people at risk from starvation. Save the Children managed to distribute food to 230,000 people, where there were alarming rates of malnutrition. They also managed to support health centres and nutritional centres to help babies and children under the age of five.

NGOs can raise a great deal of money and raise public awareness of global issues. The money can then be used to fund projects and put pressure on governments to provide further assistance. Beat Poverty is Save the Children's campaign to raise awareness of, and fight, child poverty. They are hoping to encourage governments to increase their aid budgets to the UN target of 0.7% of GNP. The UK's aid budget is increasing but it is still well below the level recommended by the UN.

What are the arguments against NGOs providing aid to the people of Africa?

Sometimes, NGOs do not have enough money to run the programmes that are needed to help the poorest people. This means that they will have to rely on help from other NGOs or governments. These other groups may then be able to influence who is helped and when.

Many projects have a small scale focus, helping only a small group of individuals. However, often large groups of people are faced with food shortages at the same time. This was the case with the Sudan emergency in 1998 and the floods in Mozambique when Oxfam was only able to help selected groups.

The large number of NGOs may make it more difficult for them to collect enough funds to make a difference.

✗ Some people may feel that they give too much to these organisations.
✗ The media may not give enough coverage as they may feel it is not news-worthy enough.
✗ NGO workers may have to spend more time collecting funds and less time working with people who are in need.

NGOs sometimes find it difficult to get enough people to work in certain parts of the world because of the danger that is involved. Many workers refuse to work in Somalia because of the problems caused by ongoing civil war between the local war lords.

NGOs usually have good intentions but corrupt governments and organisations often take advantage of them. For the last seven years, NGOs have been buying slaves out of captivity in war torn Sudan. They have paid Arab traders $50 per slave. Some genuine slaves have indeed been freed but in other cases corrupt officials of the Sudan People's Liberation Army (SPLA) have organised a well planned deceit. The Swiss-based charity Christian Solidarity International has bought back 64,000 slaves. However, in reality, many of the slaves are fakes, rounded up by SPLA officials to pose for the cameras.

Ethnic Minorities in the USA

(a) Distribution patterns of the main ethnic groups in the USA; reasons for these patterns; current trends.

(b) Social and economic progress: the nature and extent of social and economic inequalities and progress (with reference to employment, income, health, housing, education and law and order); the responses to inequalities by federal and state governments including the role of the courts.

(c) Political progress: the extent of political inequality and progress: the responses to political inequality including the role of federal and state governments, political parties and pressure groups; the influence of ethnic groups on the political process.

A knowledge of the Civil Rights Movement and progress made by ethnic minorities in the 1960s and 70s is implicit in informing an understanding of the study theme, but will not be specifically examined. Reference should be made to African Americans and Hispanics and, where appropriate, to other ethnic minorities.

Today's Americans

Population Trends (2001)

- The population of the USA grew from 76 million in 1900 to almost 285 million in July 2001.
- In 1900, 1 in 8 of the USA population was non-white. By 2001, the ratio was less than 1 in 4.
- Between 1980 and 2001, the white American population increased by 7.9%.
- Between 1980 and 2001, the non-white minority population increased by 88%.
- Between 1980 and 2001, the Hispanic American population doubled in size.
- By 2001, Hispanic Americans had become the largest ethnic minority in the USA.
- 28 million (10%) American residents aged 5+ speak Spanish at home. (1990 – 17 million)
- Just over 50% of Spanish speakers also speak English fluently.

What recent changes have taken place?

Figures published by the US Census Bureau show that Hispanic Americans had overtaken African Americans as the largest ethnic minority in the USA by 2001. Against a background of a general population increase of 1.2%, the number of Hispanic Americans increased by 4.7% to 37 million between April 2000 and July 2001. During the same period, the number of African Americans increased by 1.5% to 36.2 million. White Americans remained the largest single population group with an increase of 0.3% to 196.2 million – approximately 70% of all American residents. However, it should be noted that the total Hispanic population could be even larger than stated due to weaknesses in the methodology used in the 2000 USA census.

Some 2/3 of the Hispanic community is of Mexican origin. Many enter the USA illegally and take extraordinary risks to do so. In the last three months of 2002, more than 20 illegal immigrants died trying to cross the border from Mexico.

Population of the USA (July 2001)

Asian Americans
11.0m

White Americans
196.2m

Hispanic Americans
37.0m

Native Americans
3.2m

African Americans
36.2m

Others
1.2m

% Increases in the Population of the USA by Race (April 2000 – July 2001)

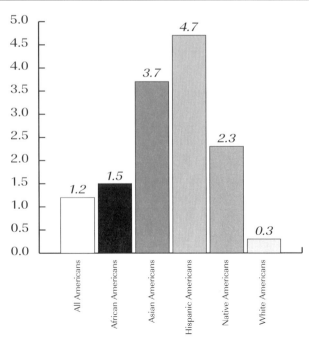

All Americans: 1.2
African Americans: 1.5
Asian Americans: 3.7
Hispanic Americans: 4.7
Native Americans: 2.3
White Americans: 0.3

Ethnic Minorities in the USA

Why have these changes taken place?

The increase in the Hispanic population is attributed to two key factors:

◆ Higher birth rates - Hispanic women, on average, give birth to three children compared to 2.1 children for African American and non-Hispanic white women.
◆ Rising immigration amongst Hispanic Americans - the economic boom of the 1990s led to many new arrivals settling in the South and Mid-West which previously had small Hispanic populations. For example, Tennessee, Georgia and North Carolina have recorded significant increases in their Hispanic populations. The signing of the North American Free Trade Agreement in 1994 by the USA, Canada and Mexico not only created the world's largest free trade zone but also led to an influx of migrants from Mexico to the USA.

These are trends which are expected to accelerate in the future.

What are the likely effects of these changes?

This significant change in the demographic make-up of the US population is likely to have a profound effect on America's political, economic and cultural landscape, with increasing evidence of the 'Latinisation' of American society.

Political changes

◆ During the 2002 election for the governor of Texas, the two leading Democratic candidates debated in Spanish in an attempt to win support from Hispanic voters.
◆ Many Hispanics continue to fail to register to vote.
◆ The low Hispanic turnout at elections continues to undermine their political power.
◆ In January 2004, President Bush announced plans to grant legal status to millions of illegal immigrants.

Economic and cultural changes

◆ In Los Angeles, many Hispanics can only find manual or menial work in order to earn a living.
◆ In Los Angeles, hundreds of Hispanics can be found outside home improvement stores offering their services in return for the minimum hourly wage.
◆ In Los Angeles, many parts of the city have become heavily dependent on casual Hispanic labour – gardeners, maids, nannies etc.
◆ In January 2003, three English-speaking radio stations in Chicago were sold to a Hispanic radio station.
◆ In Chicago, a new television station has started broadcasting in Spanish.
◆ In economic terms, the combined spending power of the Hispanic population is now estimated at $400 billion.

◆ Hispanics are now the predominant minority in many urban areas outnumbering African Americans in former black urban areas, for example in Miami and Dade County in Florida.

The Immigration Debate

The USA is a nation of immigrants. Many people moved legally to the USA during the nineteenth and twentieth centuries because of the range of opportunities that were available to them there. For many immigrants, emigration to the USA involved taking major risks in order to improve their families' standard of living. The contributions made by these individuals have helped to make the USA the successful nation it is today.

What factors influence immigration?

There are 'push' factors which force immigrants to leave their country of origin. These may include problems such as poverty, war, and political or religious persecution.

There are also 'pull' factors which attract immigrants to seek a new life in the USA.

◆ Immigrants are attracted to the USA by the prospect of achieving the 'American Dream'.
◆ Immigrants are attracted to the USA by the democratic political system.
◆ Immigrants are attracted to the USA by the the climate.
◆ Immigrants are attracted to the USA by the opportunity of a new way of life.
◆ Most (75%) legal immigrants come to join close family members.

More recently, there has been a trend for skilled/wealthy immigrants to enter the USA in the hope of further improving their standard of living.

Where do immigrants come from?

Today, many immigrants still see the USA as a land of opportunity. Each year, approximately 1 million immigrants enter the USA, legally or illegally. While some 75% of immigrants enter the USA legally, many others do so illegally.

In 1998, almost 0.75 million immigrants arrived in the USA legally and were granted permanent residence. Of these, 133,000 were refugees, asylum seekers or others fleeing persecution.

Many illegal immigrants do not come to the USA by crossing a border illegally. In fact, 40% of 'illegals' enter the USA legally with temporary student, tourist or business visas and become 'illegal' when they stay in the USA after their visa expires.

In 2002, the US Census Bureau estimated that 32.5 million people representing 11.5% of the US population were born outside of the USA. Of this total, 52% were born in Latin America, 26% in Asia, 14% in Europe and the remaining 8% in other areas of the world such as Africa and Oceania.

Foreign Born Population in the USA (Census Bureau Estimates)

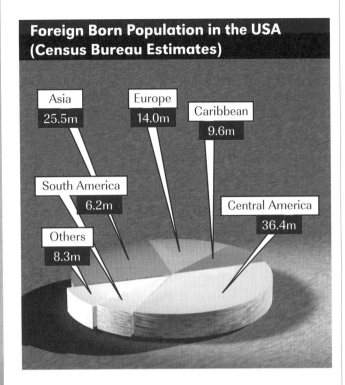

Asia 25.5m
Europe 14.0m
Caribbean 9.6m
South America 6.2m
Central America 36.4m
Others 8.3m

◆ People from Central America and Mexico accounted for more than 2/3 of the foreign-born population from Latin America. 55% of these were concentrated in the West of the USA while 30% lived in the South.

◆ Nearly half of the 32.5 million people born outside of the USA had entered the country since 1990 and more than a third of the total had become naturalised American citizens.

◆ People born in Asia and Europe had poverty rates similar to those of the native population, while people born in Central America had higher rates of poverty.

◆ Foreign-born people were more likely to live in urban areas (43%) than the native population (27%).

◆ Slightly more than 1 in 4 of the foreign-born population had a university degree – similar to the figures for the native population.

◆ More than 1 in 5 of the foreign-born population had less than a ninth grade education compared to 1 in 20 of the native population.

◆ 40% of foreign-born workers from Asia, from Europe and from Africa and Oceania were employed in managerial or professional occupations.

◆ Only 7% of foreign-born workers from Central America were employed in managerial or professional occupations.

Legal Immigration - Top Ten Countries

1	Mexico
2	China
3	India
4	Philippines
5	Dominican Republic
6	Vietnam
7	Cuba
8	Jamaica
9	El Salvador
10	Korea

Refugees - Top Ten Countries

1	Bosnia and Herzegovina
2	Former USSR
3	Vietnam
4	Somalia
5	Iran
6	Cuba
7	Liberia
8	Iraq
9	Sudan
10	Burma

What are the arguments in favour of immigration?

Many American employers depend on the supply of cheap labour provided by illegal immigrants. If industry cannot employ cheap immigrant labour, business may suffer and foreign firms may take over markets from American companies.

In the South, for example, many agricultural businesses depend on cheap labour to harvest crops. Farmers cannot afford to employ American citizens as they would have to pay them the minimum wage. Paying higher wages would increase business costs and consequently the price of goods, and many consumers would end up paying more for their agricultural products.

The authorities do acknowledge that immigrants have a positive impact on the economy of the USA.

✓ It is being made easier for illegal immigrants to settle in the USA.
✓ Immigrants can now declare their 'illegal' status without risk of deportation from the USA.
✓ Some councils, for example Los Angeles, want illegal immigrants to be allowed driving licences, safe housing, protection under the law and health care.

If immigrants were to be prevented from moving to America, not only would many people be deprived of the opportunity to improve their own circumstances but it would also damage the prospects for the American economy. Immigrants are needed to ensure that the USA continues to prosper. Immigrants may struggle in the short term but in the long run they often achieve a higher standard of living than many native born Americans.

What are the arguments against more immigration into the USA?

The percentage of Americans wanting to see a reduction in immigration has increased in recent years from 41% to 58%. This shows that the US government cannot just ignore the problem of immigration.

Many Americans argue that immigrants do not mix well with the people who already live in the USA. They say that immigrants may work alongside other racial groups but will tend to live in residential areas with their own ethnic grouping. Some Americans might suggest that immigrants who want to live in the USA should learn to live like other Americans and share their customs and beliefs.

Republicans in Congress have called for limitations on immigration. As a result, Congress passed a Welfare Act that stopped illegal immigrants gaining welfare benefits and employed more people to patrol the border with Mexico. Republicans argue that immigrants cost the American taxpayers too much money that could be spent better elsewhere. To back up this point, Republicans argue that unemployment levels amongst immigrant groups are higher than for those native born citizens of the USA. Republicans hope that this hard line anti-immigration stance will secure them more electoral support.

For many years, the immigration debate was not a significant issue for most Americans. However, the recession of the early 1990s led to higher levels of unemployment. Many unemployed Americans, rightly or wrongly, resented the fact that new immigrants had 'taken' their jobs. This matter was made worse by media sensationalisation of the issue.

Furthermore, many immigrants do not have the skills necessary to work in a highly industrialised country. When they do find work, it is often of an unskilled nature. This makes life difficult for the poorest sectors of American society, as poor Americans will be competing against immigrants for the same jobs. It is therefore likely that the poor in American society will be more against immigration than any other group because they have more to lose.

The people of California voted for Proposition 187, which stopped illegal immigrants from accessing basic services such as health and education. This, however, was declared unconstitutional by the Supreme Court but does show that stricter immigration laws have popular support in certain parts of the USA.

The Bush Administration is planning to hire an extra 1000 border police over the next five years to help patrol the border with Mexico. However, Bush has also stated that common sense and fairness dictate that US law should allow willing workers to enter the country and fill jobs that Amercans are not filling.

Asian Americans CASE STUDY

Families

There are 2.6 million Asian American families living in the USA.

80% of Asian American families consist of married couples.

54% of Asian American families include children under the age of 18.

46% of Asian American families are married couples with children under the age of 18.

Housing

55% of Asian Americans own their own home.

Education

87% of Asian Americans aged 25+ have a high school diploma.

47% of Asian Americans aged 25+ have a university degree or higher.

Income and Poverty

The average income of Asian American households is $53,635.

The poverty rate for Asian Americans is 10.2%.

1.25 million Asian Americans live in poverty.

(May 2003)

African Americans CASE STUDY

Families

There are 8.4 million African American families living in the USA.

46% of African American families consist of married couples.

56% of African American families include children under the age of 18.

24% of African American families are married couples with children under the age of 18.

Housing

46% of African Americans own their own home.

Education

72% of African Americans aged 25+ have a high school diploma.

17% of African Americans aged 25+ have a university degree or higher.

Income and Poverty

The average income of African American households is $29,470.

The poverty rate for African Americans is 22.7%.

8.1 milllion African Americans live in poverty.

(January 2003)

Hispanic Americans CASE STUDY

Families

There are 7.4 million Hispanic American families living in the USA.

67% of Hispanic American families consist of married couples.

64% of Hispanic American families include children under the age of 18.

45% of Hispanic American families are married couples with children under the age of 18.

Housing

46% of Hispanic Americans own their own home.

Education

57% of Hispanic Americans aged 25+ have a high school diploma.

11% of Hispanic Americans aged 25+ have a university degree or higher.

Income and Poverty

The average income of Hispanic American households is $33,455.

The poverty rate for Hispanic Americans is 21.2%.

7.2 milllion Hispanic Americans live in poverty.

(September 2002)

Native Americans CASE STUDY

Families

There are 936,000 Native American families living in the USA.

63% of Native American families consist of married couples.

56% of Native American families include children under the age of 18.

33% of Native American families are married couples with children under the age of 18.

Housing

55% of Native Americans own their own home.

Education

71% of Native Americans aged 25+ have a high school diploma.

11% of Native Americans aged 25+ have a university degree or higher.

Income and Poverty

The average income of Native American households is $32,116.

The poverty rate for Native Americans is 24.5%.

800,000 Native Americans live in poverty.

(November 2002)

Social and Economic Progress

What social and economic progress have ethnic minorities in the USA made?

The USA is arguably the wealthiest country in the world. However, if you scratch the surface, it is clear that many citizens do not enjoy a high standard of living. There are large variations both within and between different ethnics groups.

Education

The proportion of adults aged 25+ graduating from high school reached 84.1% in March 2002. White Americans have the highest proportion of high school graduates (88.7%), followed by Asian Americans (87.4%), African Americans (78.7%) and Hispanic Americans (57.0%).

Over the period March 2001 – March 2002, there was an overall increase of 1% in the proportion of university graduates, taking the figure to 26.7% of adults aged 25+. This resulted from significant increases in the figures for both white and African Americans. Asian Americans continue to have the highest proportion of university graduates (47.2%), followed by white Americans (29.4%), African Americans (17%) and Hispanic Americans (11.1%).

Income

More than 50% of African American families live in poverty, the comparable figure for whites being 25%. However, this does represent an improvement from 99% of African American families living in poverty in the early 1940s. More

African Americans are working in top professional jobs in law and medicine but are more likely to be found in the less lucrative professional jobs like teaching, nursing or social work. African Americans are also more likely to work for the government than other racial groups. Even though one third of African Americans may be in the middle class by profession, they are not found in the best-paid jobs to the same degree as whites.

African American families are more likely to live in poverty than any other ethnic group. In 1997, 26.5% of African American families were below the poverty line. This compares to about 10% of white families and about 30% of Hispanic families. African Americans are also four times more likely than whites to be receiving benefits like Medicaid. On average, African American workers receive about 66% of the wage of an average white person. The average income for African Americans is improving but not as quickly as the increases amongst the richest sections of the population (mainly white).

In the 1990s, about 46% of all African American households were run by single women, with the majority of these households living below the poverty line. This was more than double the figures for white households.

Many African Americans do not receive a proper education. A poor or incomplete education greatly reduces the chance of acquiring a good job. This may be reflected in the fact that, in 1995, the average income of African American families was $25,000 while for white families it was more than $40,000.

Crime

African Americans are more likely to be both the victims and the perpetrators of crime. Almost half of all homicide victims in the USA are African American, with the majority of these crimes also being carried out by African Americans. In 1998, 3,067 murders of African Americans were carried out by African Americans while 449 whites were murdered by African Americans. This would suggest that 'black-on-black' crime is a major problem in American society and that violent crime is not race-related.

Health

African Americans have higher death rates from cancer than members of other ethnic groups. African American males (life expectancy 67 years) are likely to live five years less than white males (life expectancy 72 years). In some urban areas, life expectancy for African American males is as low as 45 years. The major cause of early death in urban areas is frequently associated with violence. Infant mortality rates for African Americans are about double the rate for whites.

Affirmative Action

What is Affirmative Action?

Affirmative Action is a form of 'positive discrimination'. It was designed to give people who have faced discrimination in education, employment, health or housing a better opportunity to access a proper education, a good job, better healthcare or improved housing. Business and education were encouraged to hire and admit people from certain disadvantaged groups, particularly ethnic minorities.

What are the arguments for Affirmative Action?

Affirmative Action programmes are designed to ensure that all Americans, regardless of their ethnic origin, can achieve the 'American Dream' – if you work hard you can make a success of your life. Racism still exists in the USA even if some progress has been made. Thus, there is still a need to ensure that all Americans are given the chance to make social and economic progress. If Affirmative Action was to be declared illegal, then the progress made in the past may be lost.

Affirmative Action has helped to bring ethnic minorities into the mainstream of the American way of life by allowing people from an ethnic minority background to gain employment and access education. This should not only help to improve the overall quality of the American labour force but also help American businesses to be more successful.

As some ethnic minorities achieve success through Affirmative Action, it is hoped that they will become positive role models for younger members of their ethnic group. As more and more ethnic minorities start to believe that they can make progress, more will stay on longer at all stages of the education system. This can only help the American economy to become stronger, which can only be good for the USA as a whole.

Many people argue that Affirmative Action has been a success. More than one third of African Americans are now classified as middle class. Without Affirmative Action programmes, this would never have been possible.

Many also argue that Affirmative Action was needed to right the wrongs of the past. The history of race relations in America suggests that ethnic minorities have been exploited to the advantage of whites. The only way to redress the balance is to give the present minority population the opportunity to make up lost ground through participation in education and in employment.

What are the arguments against Affirmative Action?

Many whites argue that Affirmative Action programmes should be scrapped. They do not see why better qualified white people should lose out on jobs or places at college or university to poorer qualified African or Hispanic Americans. Some whites are particularly resentful of new immigrants who, they believe, have done little to contribute to American society. They would argue that Affirmative Action simply results in a 'self fulfilling prophecy', whereby non-white immigrants will see themselves as being discriminated against from day one. They may then start to believe that they too have a right to extra help from the government.

Some whites see the policy of Affirmative Action as a form of reverse discrimination whereby whites miss out on employment and educational opportunities even though they may be better qualified or have more experience. They do not see why the present generation of people should be expected to pay for the sins of previous generations. Even if poor whites are expected to pay the price.

Some whites would also argue that a much fairer system needs to be introduced that will encourage all sections of society to make progress.

George W Bush, President of the USA

Political Progress

What political progress have ethnic minorities in the USA made?

Hispanic American progress

In recent years, there has been a large increase in Hispanic participation in politics, including an increase in the number of candidates from Hispanic communities. As the size of the Hispanic population grows as a percentage of the total population, their influence in politics continues to rise. In states like California, the number of voters increased by more than one million during the 1990s. Many of these new voters were from ethnic minority communities.

The number of elected representatives from ethnic minority groups has also increased dramatically. In the USA as a whole, the number of elected officials from the Hispanic community has increased to more than 5,200 including 19 members of Congress. The vast majority of these are elected from those states which share a border with Mexico, as most of the Hispanic population lives in these areas of the USA. As the number of Hispanics is increasing at a quicker rate than other ethnic groups, it is likely that their influence in politics will continue to increase. There are 14 states with no elected Hispanic officials

African American progress

The number of African Americans elected to Congress is on the increase. In 1990, there were 25 elected African Americans, which was 4.7% of the total. However, by 2001, there were 39 African Americans, which was 7.3% of the total. This is obviously a sign of progress. African Americans are not very well represented in the Republican Party. This reflects the relatively small number of African American voters who support Republican candidates in elections.

The percentage of African American voters is increasing. In the 1960s, African Americans made up about 10% of the electorate but, by 1998, this had increased to about 12 %. This closely reflects the percentage of African Americans in the population as a whole.

Racial redistricting has helped to increase the representation of African Americans and Hispanics in American politics. The redrawing of electoral boundaries to create districts with predominantly ethnic minority electorates has increased opportunities for African and Hispanic American candidates. As most voters in these districts are African American or Hispanic, political parties are more willing to select an African American or Hispanic candidate, as they believe they will have a greater chance of being successful.

In recent years, more and more white voters have been willing to vote for African American or Hispanic candidates (so-called crossover candidates). This may suggest that racial attitudes are changing and candidates will be supported on the basis of their beliefs rather than their colour. By January 2000, there were a total of 9,001 elected African American officials although there were 7 states with no elected African American officials at all.

What evidence is there to suggest that ethnic minorities have not made political progress?

There has never been an African American or Hispanic president of the USA. Indeed, the Republicans and Democrats have never even selected an African American or Hispanic as their presidential candidate. However, polls have suggested that voters would vote for General Colin Powell if he were ever to stand for office.

To do well in American politics, a candidate needs to have, or be backed by, a lot of money. As African Americans are under-represented in the richest group of Americans, they may find it very difficult to get the financial backing required to run a national election campaign.

African Americans make up about 12% of the population but only 1.5% of the elected officials. They may be making some progress but they are still a long way from equality.

Most African American and Hispanic representatives are selected at local level. However, when they do get elected, they find it difficult to make progress, as many of the other representatives are white and make it difficult for the African Americans or Hispanics to make the changes they want.

The 2000 Presidential Election

Voting Statistics

In the 2000 presidential election, white Americans constituted 78% of those who were eligible to vote (ie the voting age population), African Americans 12%, Hispanic Americans 7% and others (Asian and Native Americans) 3%. The likelihood of voting differed amongst different ethnic groups. The turnout for white Americans was 62% compared to 57% for African Americans, 45% for Hispanic Americans and 43% for others.

Between 1996 and 2000, voting rates for white Americans increased by 1%, while voting rates for African Americans increased by 4%. The voting rates for Hispanic Americans and others did not change significantly at all, although the actual number of voters in both these groups increased by about 20%, reflecting the increase in the voting age population in these two groups.

The percentage of the voting age population who were registered to vote in the 2000 election was at an all time low of 64%, although, because of the overall increase in the voting age population, more people (130 million) were registered for voting than ever before. In 2000, white Americans had the highest registration rate at 72%, African Americans 68%, Hispanic Americans 57% and others (Asian and Native Americans) 52%. Among those registered to vote, 86% of white Americans actually voted followed by 84% of African Americans, 83% of others and 79% of Hispanic Americans.

Voting and Registration by Ethnic Group (November 1996 and 2000)

Ethnic Group	Percent reported registered	Percent reported voted
2000		
White	71.6	86.4
African American	67.5	84.2
Hispanic	57.3	78.6
Others	52.4	82.8
1996		
White	73.0	83.2
African Amercian	66.4	79.8
Hispanic	58.6	75.0
Others	57.2	78.8

Source: US. Census Bureau, Current Population Survey, November 2000 and 1996

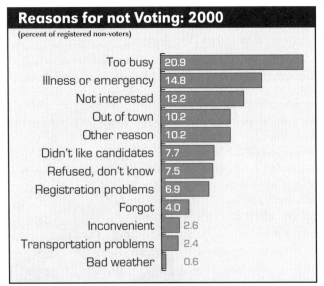

Voting in Presidential Elections : 1968 to 2000

(population 18 and older, in millions)

■ Number voted   □ Number registered but not voting

2000	1996	1992	1988	1984	1980	1976	1972	1968
18.70	22.60	12.70	16.40	14.20	12.00	11.10	12.70	7.60
110.80	105.00	113.90	102.20	101.90	93.10	86.70	85.80	79.00

Percent of registered voters voting

| 85.5 | 82.3 | 90.0 | 86.2 | 87.7 | 88.6 | 87.7 | 87.1 | 91.2 |

Reasons for not Voting: 2000

(percent of registered non-voters)

Too busy	20.9
Illness or emergency	14.8
Not interested	12.2
Out of town	10.2
Other reason	10.2
Didn't like candidates	7.7
Refused, don't know	7.5
Registration problems	6.9
Forgot	4.0
Inconvenient	2.6
Transportation problems	2.4
Bad weather	0.6

Why do some people not vote?

130 million Americans of all races were registered to vote in the 2000 presidential election. Of the19 million (14% of registered voters) who did not actually vote:

- 21% reported that they were too busy or had conflicting work or school schedules.
- 15% reported that they did not vote because they were ill, disabled or had a family emergency.
- 12% did not vote because they were not interested or felt that their vote would not make a difference.
- 10% did not vote because they were out of town on the day of the election.
- 8% did not vote because they did not like any of the candidates or campaign issues.
- 7% did not vote because of registration problems.
- 4% did not vote because they forgot.
- 3% did not vote because it was inconvenient.
- 2% did not vote because of transport problems.
- 1% did not vote because of bad weather.
- 10% did not vote because of other reasons.
- 8% refused to say or did not know why they did not vote.

Too busy?

Hispanic Americans were more likely to report that they did not vote because they were too busy or had conflicting work or school schedules.

White and African Americans were less likely to report that they did not vote because they were too busy or had conflicting work or school schedules.

Don't like the candidates?

White Americans were more likely to report that they did not vote because they did not like any of the candidates or campaign issues.

African Americans and Hispanic Americans were less likely to report that they did not like any of the candidates or campaign issues.

Transport problems?

African Americans were more likely to report that they did not vote because they had transport problems. White and Hispanic Americans were less likely to report that they did not vote because they had transport problems.

Voting by Race (1968 – 2000)

	1968	1972	1976	1980	1984	1988	1992	1996	2000
White	69.1	64.5	60.9	60.9	61.4	59.1	63.6	56.0	56.4
African American	57.6	52.1	48.7	50.5	55.8	51.5	54.0	50.6	53.5
Hispanic American	na	37.5	31.8	29.9	32.6	28.8	28.9	26.7	27.5

Source: Census Bureau – September 2001

A Society in Change – South Africa

(a) The changing structure of South African society: racial composition; settlement patterns; legacy of apartheid (with reference to income; employment; health; housing; education; crime and law and order).

(b) A political system in transition: the federal political structure since 1994; participation and representation in the democratic political system; the search for justice and reconciliation; the desire for autonomy by different groups within South Africa.

(c) Social and economic progress: the extent of social and economic problems facing South Africa; the response of governments to these problems and the consequences for different groups.

The Legacy of Apartheid

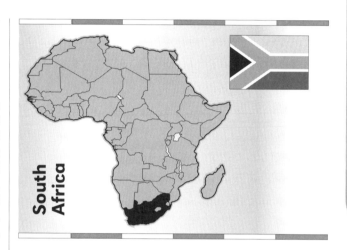

South Africa

South Africa is geographically immense. The country has a population of 46.4 million and a total land area of 1,219,000 square kilometres. Also, it is blessed with abundant mineral resources which have attracted migrants and settlers. Modern technology has supported deep mining and this has resulted in the exploitation of South Africa's vast quantities of gold, platinum, diamonds, copper, chrome and uranium. As well as being the world's major producer of all of those minerals, South Africa also provides significant quantities of asbestos, coal, copper, iron, nickel, phosphates, silver and zinc.

Despite this immense wealth, the majority of South Africans derived little benefit, as the white minority population controlled the state. Through the operation of the racist system of 'apartheid', the majority black population of South Africa obtained limited advantage from the country's prosperity and black people were denied basic human rights. Consequently, the black population of the country had to endure grinding poverty that manifested itself in low wages, oppressive housing conditions and very low standards of health care and education.

Finally, in 1994, the unjust and undemocratic system of apartheid was brought to an end. At the end of April 1994, South Africa held its first all race, democratic elections. In scenes of tremendous emotion, hundreds of thousands of black people queued for hours to cast their first vote in a democratic election.

The African National Congress (ANC) won the election and the ANC leader, Nelson Mandela, was elected President of South Africa. However, the task facing South Africa's new black-led government was immense. The internal struggle against apartheid and the effects of international sanctions against that racist system had severely damaged the South African economy. When apartheid ended in 1994, 87 per cent of South Africa's land was in the hands of just 12 per cent of the population. Eight million of the country's black citizens were living in the squalor of squatter shacks. According to the Standing Committee on Water Supply and Sanitation, 16 million people had no access to running water, 21 million had no adequate sanitation and 23 million had no access to electricity.

The Development Board of South Africa (DBSA) estimated that, in 1993, there were some 18 million people living below the Minimum Living Level (MLL) of R750 per month while between 8 and 9 million people were completely destitute (without funds to provide the basic necessities of food and shelter).

Forty six per cent of South Africans were unemployed. In addition, forty two per cent of the population were under fourteen years of age. This resulted in the workforce growing at the fast rate of 2.8 per cent each year. It was estimated that the South African economy would have to grow by, at least, 4.5 per cent each year just to prevent any further increase in unemployment.

The education system had virtually collapsed. Sixty per cent of the population was illiterate and the failure rate of those young black people attending school was alarming. In 1994, it was established that South Africa had one of the world's highest murder rates for a country not at war. Compared to a world average of 5.5 murders per 100,000 people, South Africa's murder rate was 45 murders per 100,000.

Furthermore, expectations were at an all time high. The black population, crushed by long decades of apartheid, was expecting a quick result from democratic elections and black majority rule in the form of jobs, houses and decent schools.

It is in the context of the crushing legacy of the racist system of apartheid, as evidenced by the above statistics that the achievements of the ANC led government and its political allies must be viewed.

The ANC in Government (1994-2003): Social and Economic Progress

In 1997, the leader of the ANC, Nelson Mandela, stood down from this position and was replaced by his deputy Thabo Mbeki. In 1999, the ANC was re-elected as the government of South Africa and Thabo Mbeki became the new President of South Africa. The next South African general election will take place in April 2004. It will coincide with the celebration of ten years of democracy.

It seems almost certain that the ANC will easily win the 2004 general election and that Thabo Mbeki will be re-elected as President. Nonetheless, some opinion polls suggest that a significant number of black voters have become disenchanted by the amount of progress made by the ANC-led government and suggest that apathy has set in, to the extent that some may not bother to cast their vote at all.

In analysing the economic progress made by the government, it is possible to provide the following summary. Progress has been made in providing basic services including water, sanitation, housing and improved access to health care and education. In addition, the land redistribution programme has made headway. The net result of this is that, in general, South Africans are a little better off, better educated, better housed and have better access to health care and hygiene than they had a decade ago. Also, the population has risen from 40.5 million in 1994 to 46.4 million in 2003. People have more material possessions such as telephones, radios, televisions, cars and refrigerators.

However, despite this impressive progress, there are a number of noted areas of concern. Firstly, unemployment continues to exist at an unacceptable level. It is consistently estimated that the true level of unemployment in South Africa is around 40 per cent. This contrasts with an official unemployment rate of 25 per cent. Education and skills training are generally considered to be failing to keep pace with the rapid increase in demand for skilled workers. Furthermore, the South African economy is being adversely affected by the loss of skilled white workers. The October 2001 census notes the white population as having fallen from 10.9 per cent in 1996 to 9.6 per cent. Unofficial figures place white emigration at a much higher level.

Concern is also expressed that insufficient economic improvement is being made, and that the progress which is being made is not reaching all of the population. For example, it is estimated that of black people, one in two does not have a job and noted that poor provinces such as the Eastern Cape have failed to benefit from any rise in prosperity.

Furthermore, a black middle class has developed which has benefited from the ANC's policies of Africanisation and Affirmative Action. Affirmative Action is about ensuring a significant black presence at every level of government departments and public institutions. The government has also been successful in promoting the development of black owned businesses. The South African government is able to use its powerful position as a major purchaser and supplier to promote the interests of black owned businesses and black people through the Black Economic Empowerment (BEE) programme.

These government initiatives have led to a significantly higher standard of living for a small minority of black people

Thabo Mbeki

and this is viewed as necessary to support continuing economic development. However, many black people are concerned that the racial inequalities that they had to endure under apartheid are now being replaced by social class inequalities. The increase in income per head of population to $3,310 in 2003 disguises the fact that many black people have derived little benefit from this. There is concern within the ANC that, should the situation not improve, impoverished black South Africans might switch their support to more radical political parties.

The main economic strategy pursued by the ANC-led government since 1996 has been GEAR (Growth, Employment and Redistribution Strategy). This plan to promote economic growth established a number of targets:

(a) Encourage foreign investment

The government has attempted to strictly control public spending in order to attract foreign investment. This has made it more difficult for South Africa to meet the expectations of its citizens and has led to accusations that the government is failing to make adequate progress. However, since 1994, a large number of European and American firms have invested in South Africa and the US is the largest source of foreign investment. Foreign investment has been a major cause of the economic growth rate rising to 3.5 per cent in 2003.

Foreign investment has also been encouraged by Thabo Mbeki's policies of eliminating most foreign exchange controls, reducing import tariffs and privatising state owned assets.

(b) Moderation of trade union wage demands

The government has attempted to put in place an economic system which generates job security, decent wages and appropriate working conditions. To achieve this, it has removed the restrictions on workers and trade unions that existed under apartheid. Workers now have the right to strike, a 45 hour working week has been established, Affirmative Action policies have been put in place to secure the employment of black people and employers are required to spend one per cent of their payroll costs on training programmes.

Nevertheless, despite this progress COSATU (the Congress of South African Trade Unions) remains concerned about the exploitation of workers through the low wages associated with part-time, casual and unskilled work.

(c) Privatisation of publicly owned businesses and utilities

Since November 1999, President Mbeki has made privatisation a vital element of the country's economic strategy. A programme to privatise the 'big four' state businesses, Denel (defence), Eskom (electricity), Transnet (transportation) and Telkom (telecommunications) has been implemented. It is anticipated that the privatisation programme will stimulate further significant foreign investment during the course of 2004.

The Affirmative Action programme has been stepped up in recognition of the criticism that the government is failing to tackle unemployment as a root cause of the continuing poverty of the majority of the black population. During 2004, a new law will take effect, requiring all firms needing a government operating licence or undertaking government contracts to demonstrate that their recruitment and training of black people is fair and equitable.

Maintaining Political Stability in South Africa (1994-2003)

South Africa's first democratic, multi-racial elections took place in April 1994. Voting took place between April 26th and 28th 1994. In scenes of tremendous emotion, hundreds of thousands of black people queued for hours in glorious Spring weather to cast their first vote in a democratic election.

Despite some evidence of intimidation, particularly in the fraught province of Kwa-Zulu Natal, the Independent Electoral Commission (IEC) set up to conduct the election declared it to be "substantially free and fair". The ANC won 62.7% of the vote. On May 10th 1994, Nelson Mandela took the presidential oath.

In his inauguration speech, he swore that, "never again shall it be that this beautiful country will again experience the oppression of one by another." In this spirit of hope and optimism South Africa embarked on its new democratic future.

The euphoria generated by the election of President Nelson Mandela and the ANC-led Government of National Unity served to provide a brief respite from the reality of South Africa's deep-rooted social and economic problems. In May 1994, opinion polls revealed that 76 per cent of South Africans were satisfied with the overall political situation in the country.

However, the task facing South Africa's new black-led, democratic government in 1994 was immense. The South African economy had been ravaged by the struggle against apartheid and the effects of sanctions. As a result, a severe economic recession had been experienced, although some improvement had been noted in 1993-94 as the first democratic election approached and optimism grew.

The new South African government undertook its responsibilities with great energy and drive. The joy created by the success of South Africa's first democratic elections was soon replaced by hard-headed realism, as the government got down to the complex task of building the new South Africa.

Nelson Mandela

The main challenges that faced the Government of National Unity were as follows:

◆ To maintain political stability and prevent the development of unrest and possible civil war. This involved a delicate balancing act to ensure that the some of the aspirations of each of the main interest groups within South Africa were met;

◆ To put in place a social and economic development programme capable of tackling the deep-seated poverty afflicting black South Africans. The vital components of this programme were the creation of employment opportunities, house building, land reform and improvements in the provision of education and health care;

◆ To ensure that the development programme which was put in place did not result in very high levels of taxation which would act as a disincentive to foreign investment or encourage skilled white workers to emigrate;

◆ To take steps to make South Africa a more cohesive society. This involved redressing the impact of racism by providing more opportunities for black people to advance their position within society. However, it was also necessary to reassure the 5 million whites, 3.5 million Coloureds and 1 million Indians living in the country that they would not lose out as a result of steps taken to improve living conditions for the black majority;

◆ To tackle the crime wave problem that had the effect of generating insecurity and instability. It was necessary for the new government to build confidence and demonstrate that it was fully in control.

It was against this background that the South African government had to manage the country's transformation from a racially exclusive apartheid regime to a constitutional democracy based on the rule of law and the protection of human rights.

During his five years as president of South Africa (1994-1999), Nelson Mandela was successful in maintaining and reinforcing political stability within the divided nation and raising the profile of South Africa in international affairs.

Prior to the 1994 elections, South Africa was generally considered to be on the verge of civil war. White right-wingers threatened to overthrow Mandela's ANC-led government and significant tension existed between supporters of the ANC and

the Zulu dominated Inkatha Freedom Party. These elements of political instability combined with the challenges presented by poverty and the economy to generate a pessimistic outlook for the new government. Mandela's lasting achievement is that he was able to retain the support of the great majority of South African people.

This fact was reflected by the 1999 national election in which the ANC recorded another resounding victory. In this general election, the African National Congress gained 266 National Assembly seats. The number of seats won by the other major parties were as follows; the Democratic Party 38, the Inkatha Freedom Party 34, the New National Party 28, the United Democratic Movement 14, and the African Christian Democratic Party 6. The remaining smaller parties obtained 14 seats between them.

Since 1999, the new President of South Africa, Thabo Mbeki has continued to attempt to promote stability by tackling the political, social and economic challenges that the country faces. In this regard, there have been some notable successes. Economic growth is projected to reach 3.5 per cent in 2004, a figure which is approaching the level required if the severe unemployment experienced within South Africa is to be reduced. Also, the government is increasing spending on social services to improve conditions for the poor. As a consequence of these developments, the ANC retains the support of much of the black population and is likely to win the 2004 general election by a significant margin.

In this regard, some fears have been expressed that the continuing strength of the ANC may lead to the development of a one-party state. The ANC already has a clear two-thirds majority in parliament, giving it power to rewrite the constitution. It may retain this powerful position after the 2004 general election is held in April.

However, it is worth noting that President Mbeki has, to date, proved skilled at enlisting and retaining the support of potential political rivals. The ANC and the Inkatha Freedom Party (IFP), led by Mangosuthu Buthelezi, have established a working relationship. Mr Buthelezi continues to hold the post of Minister of Home Affairs in the Cabinet.

Nonetheless, in recent times, Mr Buthelezi has encouraged opposition parties to form a strong coalition against the ANC to prevent the party from getting the two-thirds majority which would allow it to make changes to the constitution. To this end, the IFP has resolved to strengthen its partnership with the Democratic Alliance (DA). The Democratic Alliance was formed in the year 2000 by the amalgamation of the Democratic Party (DP) and the New National Party (NNP). The Democratic Alliance is mainly supported by whites and it enjoys the support of approximately one in five voters.

Within the ANC, traditional ties with trade union and Communist partners have been tested by Mbeki's commitment to foreign investment and privatisation. However, for as long as the economy is seen to be progressing, the influence of critics of these policies will be limited.

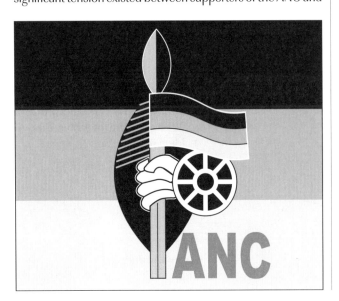

Truth and Reconciliation

The Archbishop of Cape Town and veteran anti-apartheid campaigner, Desmond Tutu, opened the proceedings of the Truth and Reconciliation Commission (TRC) as its Chairman on April 15th 1996. At that time he said,

"We are charged to unearth the truth of our dark past and to lay the ghosts of our past so that they will not return to haunt us, for all of us in South Africa are wounded people."

The Truth and Reconciliation Commission had two main functions. Victims and their families were to have long-denied recognition of their ordeals. Perpetrators, both apartheid agents and black liberation fighters, were to have the opportunity to be granted amnesty if they could demonstrate that they had been truthful and that their actions were politically motivated. In this way, it was hoped that, at the end of the two year enquiry by the Commission into human rights abuses during the period March 1960 to December 1993, South Africa would be in a position to build a brighter future, having confronted some of the most unsavoury episodes in its troubled past.

The recounting of these incidents created much bitterness and debate in South Africa. Terrible crimes were committed under apartheid. Some of the most shocking evidence to emerge from the TRC was the existence of a 'third force', an underground group of assassins and killers who were paid by the secret police to commit atrocities which could then be blamed on the ANC. Their activities included such extremes as bombing units of the South African police and army in order to make it appear that these were atrocities committed by the ANC's armed wing, MK ('Spear of the Nation').

After two years of deliberations, which included the testimony of victims and appeals for amnesty from hundreds of applicants, the TRC issued its final report at the end of October 1998. The report surveyed the human rights record of all the participants in the apartheid struggle and its conclusions produced a storm of protests from all parties. Most of the blame for atrocities committed during the apartheid era was placed firmly on the shoulders of the apartheid government of the National Party. The report detailed the systematic way the apartheid government had used the secret police to torture and kill its opponents.

Nonetheless, the major criticism made of the work of the TRC was that it had failed to deal adequately with the most senior perpetrators of atrocities. A key provision of the TRC was that those who made a full and honest confession of their works during the apartheid era would be granted amnesty. The issue of amnesty is very controversial. Some commentators argue that, without the protection afforded by amnesty, offenders would not have been prepared to come forward and the truth would never have been known. Others take the view that some of the crimes are so atrocious that the perpetrators must be punished.

One police captain, Jacques Hechter, admitted in his amnesty application that he strangled, burned, shot, kicked and blew up 25 people. He revealed that he had been involved in a total of 65 murders. Some of the details presented in evidence by him to the commission resulted in a number of participants being deeply upset.

In the face of such crimes, some victims and their families have argued that the perpetrators should be made to stand trial and claim that justice has not been served by the TRC. This understandable anger has been further fuelled by the fact that the compensation for victims and their families, promised as part of the TRC process, has been slow to arrive.

The Reparation and Rehabilitation Committee was set up to help victims obtain required medical or psychological treatment. It is also able to assist in securing pensions and ensuring that the educational needs of victims' children are provided for. In addition, the Reparation and Rehabilitation Committee can recommend symbolic recognition for victims of extraordinary suffering. This could involve a health clinic being named in remembrance of the victim or a scholarship being created in their name.

Such measures are recognised by the South African government as important steps in healing the divisions that exist within society. However, a significant problem for the government is the scale of the proposed payments. Confronted with a bill for compensation amounting to 3 billion rand (approximately £250 million), the government has actively sought to delay and reduce payments. This has added to the anger and disappointment of victims and their families.

Such was the extent of this problem that Archbishop Desmond Tutu, who chaired the TRC, claimed that the issue had the potential to destabilise South Africa. He argued that the government should levy a wealth tax on those who benefited from apartheid to fund the compensation due to victims and their families. Although President Thabo Mbeki rejected this option for fear that it may scare off foreign investors, in April 2003 he announced that the government would pay a grant of almost £2,500 to each of 19,000 victims of apartheid who had appeared before the Truth and Reconciliation Commission.

Archbishop Desmond Tutu

Challenging Social Issues

Health Care and AIDS

The South African Aids and HIV infection crisis has caused President Mbeki's leadership to be heavily criticised. In 2002, it was estimated that around 1500 people per day were being newly infected with HIV. Such is the severity of the problem that four million people are already infected and, until recently, there seemed little prospect of any decrease in the rate of infection. A recent World Bank study warned of the potential for a "complete economic collapse" in South Africa if there is no effective response to AIDS.

The statistics relating to Aids and HIV infection in South Africa are frightening. Even though approximately half of South Africa's population is aged 19 or under, projections on AIDS-related deaths show that it will decimate the working age population. Consequently, the elderly will make up an increasing proportion of South Africa's total population. Already, five million people have HIV or Aids, representing more that one in 10 of the country's 46 million people. The average life expectancy of a South African citizen has plummeted from 66 years to 47 years and it is estimated that, by 2010, seven million South Africans will have died as a direct result of AIDS.

In the face of such a crisis, the response of President Thabo Mbeki has been controversial. He has consistently blocked plans to allow universal access to anti-AIDS drugs and justified this on a range of grounds. Firstly and most controversially, he has questioned the link between HIV and AIDS and stated that he does not know of anyone suffering from AIDS. Secondly, he has expressed doubts about the safety and usefulness of drugs designed to combat HIV and AIDS (anti-retroviral drugs). Thirdly, concern has been expressed about the possible profit motives of Western producers of anti-retroviral drugs.

This latter concern is probably the most significant, and important progress has been made in recent times. In October 2003, South Africa's competition commission announced that it had accepted the case that the high charges made for Aids drugs were unfair. The commission's recommendations are likely to result in cheap anti-retroviral drugs being made available in South Africa as, in November 2003, the South African government announced its intention to distribute free anti-retroviral drugs through the health system.

Crime

In 2002, more than 21,000 people were murdered in South Africa. This was roughly the same number as in 2001. To put this figure in context, 16,110 people were murdered in the United States during the course of 2001. Many more were murdered in South Africa, despite the fact that the US population is six times the size of South Africa's.

South Africa has the highest murder rate (murders per 100,000 people) in the world. Its murder rate is ten times that of the USA and statistics for other major crimes are equally daunting. In 2002, the following crimes were reported:

- 21,000 people were murdered;
- 5,000 people were murdered in Johannesburg and Pretoria alone;
- 12,000 rapes were reported in Johannesburg;
- 168,000 people were seriously assaulted;
- 77,000 people were hi-jacked and/or robbed at gunpoint.

In reviewing this situation, some commentators have likened South African society to a war zone.

A major concern for South Africans is the low detection and conviction rate. It has been reliably estimated that only about one in 10 South African murderers end up in jail. Such is the crime rate that South African prisons are bursting at the seams with 180,000 inmates crowded into prisons built for 110,000.

Two important causes of South Africa's crime problem are the violent legacy of apartheid and the extreme social and economic inequality that exists within the country.

During the struggle against apartheid, many young men were taught to defy authority by using violence against the state and the police. Others were in the pay of police involved in 'third force' activities. Schools were boycotted and the young people involved learned to live by such criminal activities as theft and carjacking. Today, faced by high unemployment and grinding poverty, they have embraced crime as a way to survive and express anger.

This volatile situation is worsened by the activities of crime syndicates. Organised crime has moved into South Africa. This includes Japanese Yakuza gangsters specialising in financial fraud, the Nigerian mafia which controls the drug trade, Mexican cartels dealing in crack and cocaine and Chinese Triads which concentrate on gambling and contraband like rhino horn. South Africa is viewed by such groups as a land of opportunity.

Some black South Africans are moving up the socio-economic ladder and are able to purchase a lavish lifestyle that includes luxury homes, cars and designer clothes. This contrast in wealth proves too much for some young people who are prepared to use weapons to improve their lot. The high level of gun ownership in South Africa (also a legacy of the apartheid years) is a major factor fuelling the extreme crime rate. The government has experienced genuine difficulty in coping with this severe problem. It believes that its economic policies are bearing fruit by making South Africa a wealthier country, and that this will eventually serve to ensure that the blight of poverty and unemployment is removed. However, in the meantime, South Africa has the biggest differences in wealth between races and classes experienced anywhere in the developed World.

In addition, the government's attempts to tackle crime are hampered by corruption and the shortage of police officers and well-trained detectives. The police force is generally viewed as overworked and underpaid with the result that it is unable to devote the time required to solve each case. Even when caught, the overburdened justice system is slow to deal with criminals, and many escape unpunished.

There are early indications that improved police training and the increasing use of closed-circuit cameras are beginning to reduce street crime. Nonetheless, most wealthy South African city dwellers avoid walking whenever possible and spend heavily on security measures designed to protect their homes and their families.

How to Study for Higher Modern Studies

People learn in different ways. However, there are a number of common factors which will help most people.

Where to work

Try to ensure you have a place that is:

◆ quiet so that people will not disturb you.
◆ comfortable for you to work in. This might mean a large desk and chair.
◆ uncluttered but with all the equipment needed close at hand.
◆ free from distractions.
◆ well lit.

Managing your time

If you are studying for four or five Higher or Intermediate exams you may feel that you don't have enough time to study. However, if you start to revise early and manage your time carefully, there should not be a problem.
Work through the following calculation and put in your own results, as it may help you realise how much time is available.

1. How many hours are there in a week? 7×24 = 168 hours
2. How much time do you spend in class? 30×50 minutes = 25 hours
3. How long do you sleep for? 9×7 = 63 hours
4. How long do you work for?   10 hours
5. How much free time do you want each day? 2×7 = 14 hours

Total hours use = 14 + 10 + 63 + 25 = 112
168 - 112 = 56 hours

This means that you have 56 hours each week in which you could study. This would give you eight hours every day. Nobody would expect to study for this time. However, if you could do an extra two hours every day, what a difference it might make. This would still allow you to do the other things that you like doing. It would also help if you were to plan out your study times on a timetable. Your studying could be organised in such a way that you can still do all your other activities and hobbies.

Time	Monday	Tuesday	Wednesday	Thursday	Friday	Saturday	Sunday
8 – 10							
10 – 12							
12 – 2							
2 – 4							
4 – 6							
6 – 8							
8 – 10							
10 – 11							

Important
It is not a good idea to work for too long. It is better to work in short bursts. This will help improve your concentration.

Time management and the exam

The Higher Modern Studies exam is made up of two papers. In Paper 1, you have to answer five 10 mark questions. In Section A, Political Issues in the UK, you have to answer two 10 mark questions from the same Study Theme. In Section B, Social Issues in the UK, you have to answer one 10 mark question from either Study Theme 5 or Study Theme 6. In Section C, International Issues, you have to answer two 10 mark questions from the same Study Theme.

In 85 minutes you must answer five questions. This means that you can divide the time up so that you have 17 minutes per question, or give yourself 5 minutes to select the questions, 15 minutes to answer each of the 5 questions and 5 minutes to quickly check your answers. It doesn't matter which system you use.

In Paper 2, you have to complete a Decision-Making Exercise. In the exam, you will have to select **either** Decision-Making Exercise 1: Income and Wealth in the UK or Decision-Making Exercise 2: Health Care in the UK. You should answer the question from the area that you have studied in class so that you can include your own background knowledge.

You have 80 minutes to answer the short questions worth 10 marks and the Decision Making Exercise worth 20 marks. Try to think about how you will use this time before you go into the exam. A possible approach might be:

◆ read and answer short questions (20 minutes).
◆ plan report including use of all sources, your own knowledge and covering all aspects of the task (15 minutes).
◆ write a report (45 minutes).

Preparing for the examination

For the Higher Modern Studies examination, you have to learn relevant information to include in the essay questions and to include in the Decision Making Exercise. You should also practise exam questions under exam conditions.

Content of the course

To do well in Higher Modern Studies, you need to learn the facts about your chosen topics. It will also help if you can memorise up-to-date examples in order that you can develop each point further. You will find some examples in this book. However, if you watch news programmes, read

Popular Examination Topics - Paper I

POLITICS IN THE UNITED KINGDOM

STUDY THEME 1 Decision Making in Central Government

The Prime Minister (powers, limitations, changes to role) – 1994, 1996, 1997, 1998, 2001.

Influences on the government (backbench MPs, Parliament, opposition, Lords) – 1994, 1995, 1996, 1997, 2000, 2001.

Pressure groups – 1994, 1995, 1996, 1997, 1998, 1999, 2000, 2002, 2003.

STUDY THEME 2 The Government of Scotland

Impact of devolution – 1994, 1995, 1997, 1998, 1999, 2000, 2001, 2003.

Role of MSPs – 2002.

Powers of local government – 1995, 1996, 1997, 2001, 2002, 2003.

STUDY THEME 3 Political Parties and their Policies

Party organisation – 1994, 1996, 1997, 1998, 1999, 2001, 2002, 2003.

Party policies – 1994, 1996, 1997, 1998, 1999, 2001, 2002, 2003.

STUDY THEME 4 The Electoral System, Voting and Political Attitudes

First Past the Post – 1995, 1996, 1998, 2001, 2002.

Proportional representation – 1996, 1998, 1999, 2000, 2002, 2003.

Voting behaviour – 1995, 1997, 1999, 2000, 2001, 2003.

The mass media – 1996, 2002.

HEALTH CARE IN THE UNITED KINGDOM

NHS aims – 1995, 1998, 2002, 2003.

NHS reforms – 1994, 1995, 1996, 1998, 2000, 2001.

Private health care – 1995, 1997, 1998, 1999, 2000, 2002.

Inequalities in health – 1994, 1996, 1997, 1999, 2001, 2003.

The elderly – 1995, 1997, 1998, 1999, 2000, 2001, 2003.

POLITICS OF FOOD

Causes of food shortages – 1995, 1997, 1998, 1999, 2000, 2001, 2002, 2003.

Bilateral aid – 1994, 2000.

NGOs – 1997, 1999, 2001.

Specialised agencies – 1995, 1996, 1998, 2002, 2003.

ETHNIC MINORITIES IN THE USA

Immigration – 2003.

Population distribution – 1996, 1999, 2001.

Social and economic progress – 1994, 1995, 1996, 1997, 1998, 2000, 2002.

Affirmative Action – 1995, 1997, 1999, 2001, 2003.

Political progress – 1994, 1995, 1996, 1997, 1998, 2000, 2002.

A SOCIETY IN CHANGE – SOUTH AFRICA

Social and economic progress – 1994, 1995, 1996, 2002.

Social and economic problems – 1997, 1998, 1999, 2000, 2001, 2002, 2003.

Political reforms – 1995, 1998, 1999, 2002, 2003.

Political problems – 1996, 2000.

relevant sections of newspapers and look up news websites then you will be able to collect more. This will help you to improve your grade in the exam.

As was stated earlier, people learn information in different ways. This section will highlight some of the methods that could be used to help you to retain all the facts. These include:

- note taking
- mind maps
- spider diagrams
- acronyms
- daft sentences.

Try to find the methods that help you best.

Note taking

In the Higher course, you will have studied a number of different topics over the year. If you were to try and remember all this information from your jotter it would be a very difficult task. However, the following hints might help to make it more manageable.

First you need to work out what you need to know. To do this, you should look at previous exam questions. It would help you to organise your notes if you put a number of key ideas / points under each of the exam questions. When you have finished this, ask someone to check that all your examples are relevant and that you have not missed any out.

Remember to check through your jotter, notebook, folder, class notes and text books. If you have 5 or 6 pieces of relevant information then you should have enough material to use in the exam. Always try to have examples to back up these points.

Mind Maps and Spider Diagrams

Note
What is important is that you answer all 5 questions in the time that you are given. Try to think about the time before you go into the exam. You must be able to explain each of these points in relation to the question that you have been asked to answer.

Some people like to make notes using spider diagrams. This helps to lay out the information more clearly.

Other students like to use Mind Maps. They are very much Spider Diagrams only they may also include colour and pictures. For some people this makes it much easier to learn.

Acronyms

Acronym - where each letter stands for a point or word.

If you were trying to remember powers of the Prime Minister you could use *pader*:
p = presentation of policy
a = appointments
d = development of policy
e = election date
r = representing the UK

Make up a silly sentence

If you are trying to remember a number of points, it may help if you try to make up a silly sentence using the first letter from each of the points. Sometimes, the sillier the sentence is, the more likely you are to remember the points.

Thus if you were again trying to remember the powers of the Prime Minister you could use: *people don't always eat rats*

This would mean:

p = presentation of policy
d = development of policy
a = appointments
e = election date
r = representing the UK

Other methods

- Record information onto a tape and play it back.
- Try to remember relevant facts and ask people to question you.
- Go for long walks and try to think important issues through.
- Record points on large pieces of paper and stick them to the wall (obviously with parents' permission).
- Type notes onto a computer.

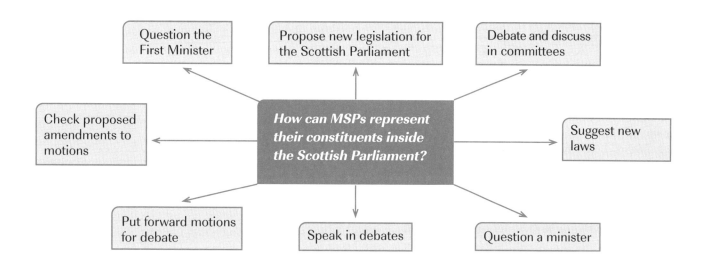

Questions under examination conditions

When you think you have learned the facts from one area of the course you should try to complete a past paper question under exam conditions. This will show you whether or not there are any gaps in your knowledge. Ask your teacher to check your work. He or she may be able to give you some advice as to how you can make a higher score.

Decision-Making Exercises (DMEs)

The best way to practise DMEs is to attempt the questions and the report under exam conditions. If you ask your teacher to mark the answers they may be willing to provide advice on how you could improve.

And then there's the examination ...

Doing as well as possible in the examination is, for most people, extremely important. There are some techniques which you can use to ensure success. Most of the following section is about how to approach the answering of questions rather than telling you what to put in them.

The Higher Modern Studies examination consists of two papers. Paper 1 is divided up into the familiar topics and consists of essay type questions. Your answers will be drawn from the material you have studied throughout your Modern Studies course.

Paper 2 is a Decision Making Exercise which asks you to write a report based on material which appears in the paper. You will also need background knowledge for this paper.

Do the simple thing! Find some past papers and clue yourself up on the requirements!

Answer the question!

You need to do two things to get the best result possible from your course. Firstly, make sure that you have followed a regular and structured revision timetable. Then make sure that the information you have available is put to the best possible use by answering the question! You will hear this advice often. It is based on the experiences of teachers who have watched their pupils achieve high grades due to following this advice.

Practise!

Many pupils who are quite happy to develop their guitar-playing, golf, hockey, or keepy-uppy skills by practising for ages don't seem to realise that practising Modern Studies questions will also bring about an improvement in performance. Your teacher will be delighted to supply you with past papers and to mark your answers. When you get successful ones back, ask your teacher why it got a good mark, then keep using the formula. Nobody knows your capabilities better than your own teacher. Ask for advice then apply it!

The first essential is to read the question. It will be quite clear from the wording of the question what subject matter you have to work with and how you have to deal with it.

An Outcome 1 Question

'Trigger' words such as 'explain', 'describe', 'in what ways', 'what evidence is there' and 'outline' signal Outcome 1 questions. These test knowledge and understanding. No introduction is necessary in Outcome 1 answers.

Example:

Describe the ways in which the Scottish Executive is accountable to the Scottish Parliament?

Your description of this issue must be accurate and make reference to factors, institutions and examples that are relevant. You may wish to explain ways in which MSPs raise matters in the Scottish Parliament. Try to make at least three points from: Question Time; making statements in the Chamber; leading debates in plenary session; scrutiny of departmental expenditure; giving evidence to committees.

No introduction is necessary in Outcome 1 answers.
For each point: state the point, explain it then give an example e.g. Question Time.

Question Time

MSPs can ask oral questions of the Ministers and the First Minister at Question Time. They can also send written questions to the Executive. Both oral and written questions and answers are recorded and made available to the public. In June 2003, Murdo Fraser (Conservative MSP for Mid Scotland and Fife) asked the Scottish Executive whether it had assessed the economic impact of reducing business rates to the same level as England. The Minister, Andy Kerr, replied that the Executive was undertaking a study to compare the levels of local taxation with Scotland's competitors in Europe.

An Outcome 2 Question

'Trigger' words such as 'to what extent', 'discuss' and 'examine' signal Outcome 2 questions. These test your ability to analyse key issues.

Some awkward key words and phrases that appear in questions:

- Discuss........ means that you have to have more than one side of an argument and/or to outline various ways of looking at an issue.
- To what extent........ asks you to judge the relative importance of a factor or factors.
- Examine the main factors....... means that you should go through the main factors, commenting on the importance of each as you go.
- Assess..... or Evaluate....... asks you to place value on the importance of something (which will very probably be mentioned later in the question).
- Justify means that you have to back up your claims with evidence.

Remember

Providing and analysing relevant evidence is the way to success in Higher Modern Studies.

Example:

To what extent are pressure groups undemocratic?

Your analysis of the issue must be balanced with relevant exemplification. It must also have a relevant and developed conclusion. The answer to this question could have four paragraphs:

1. A brief introduction

2. Examples of pressure groups being undemocratic. (such as: substantial resources and well-off members; breaking the law; leadership making decisions without approval of members.)

3. Examples of pressure groups being democratic. (such as: insider groups provide information to help the Government make informed decisions; allows minority views to be expressed; encourages individuals to participate.)

4. A relevant and developed conclusion.

Try to use words and phrases such as 'but', 'however', 'notwithstanding', 'although', 'on the other hand', 'nevertheless', 'nonetheless', 'yet', 'still', 'conversely', 'then again' when answering Outcome 2 questions. The use of such words and phrases should ensure balance.

The Decision-Making Exercise

There are two parts to this paper which lasts for one hour and twenty minutes and which is based on source material provided for you in the examination paper.

First you have to answer 10 marks worth of short-answer questions, then, for a further twenty marks, write a report.

The Short Answer (Evaluating) Questions

These questions are based entirely on sources which are included in the examination paper. These sources may cover a wide range of types, so be prepared to read articles or reports, to interpret graphs, pie-charts or histograms (bar-charts) or to work with statistical tables.

Don't be put off by the apparently long list above! The examiners are well aware that you will be working to an examination timescale, so the sources used in the paper will not be too difficult or detailed. You are also very unlikely to meet a type of source which you haven't met before.

Important points about this part of the paper:

◆ Give it your full attention. Many pupils find that they can build up high marks here.
◆ Follow the instructions in each question to the letter. Use only the sources you are directed to. Do not use the other sources. Do not bring in background knowledge at this stage.
◆ Look carefully at the direction the questions take. Treat the questions as a strong hint as to the structure your report should follow.

The Report

The Social Issues in the United Kingdom Unit

The decision-making exercise asks you to include written and / or oral evidence which satisfies all of the outcomes (outcome 1, Outcome 2 and Outcome 3). You are required to evaluate three complex sources such as a written opinion, a written factual statement, graphs and statistical tables in a relevant and accurate manner. The analysis of these must be balanced and include appropriate conclusions and points of view. You must also use relevant background knowledge.

What you have to do

You will be asked to take on a role ... often that of an adviser to the government or other public body. Then, having considered the evidence in the sources in the paper, you will be asked to produce a recommendation on which course of action should be followed. You must bring in background knowledge.

You must make a recommendation! Provided that you carry out the role you are asked to and consider all of the sources carefully and in an unbiased way, you will not be penalised because you did not make the right recommendation! A well argued combination of use of the sources and background knowledge is the key to a high mark.

How to do it

Read the sources carefully. You will find that the examiners will have provided you with more than one side of the argument. Start by deciding which sources go with which side of the argument and assemble them very quickly under headings. Then decide what recommendation you are going to make.

Now plan your answer in greater detail. Assemble your arguments in favour of your recommendation, preferably in descending order of priority.

Remember that you must refer to the sources you have been given and that you must bring in background knowledge, either to develop source-based points or to make other arguments in favour of your recommendation. Try to avoid using background material which, for example, comes from your personal or family experience as it is very unlikely to be appropriate.

Next, you need to have a serious look at the awkward sources, the ones which go against the recommendation you are making. These must not be ignored but must be recognised and included in your report. You may find that you can counter some of these arguments, but don't worry if you can't. There is nothing wrong with saying that your recommendation is made on the balance of the evidence after having taken everything into account.

Write your report. Remember that it is a report and that it should be written in straightforward language. Words such as idiotic, brilliant or numpties should not appear. Present the arguments in formal, unemotional, logical terms.

If you have been getting good marks on practice reports just keep doing what you have been doing. If you find structuring your report a struggle, try this:

◆ A short paragraph explaining your role.
◆ A short paragraph that includes a clear recommendation.
◆ A substantial paragraph which presents the arguments for your recommendation. References to the sources and inclusion of background knowledge are essential.
◆ A paragraph which addresses possible objections to, or difficulties with, your recommendation. Again, proper references are essential. Do not simply dismiss the opposing view out of hand!
◆ A final paragraph which summarises the for and against arguments and which arrives back at a restatement of your recommendation.

Student Self Assessment

Modern Studies Higher Paper 1
Homework and Classwork

Each time you write an essay you should use the following checklist to make sure that you have been as thorough as possible.

Before attempting an essay you should always:

(a)   read the question carefully;
(b)   plan the answer;
(c)   carry out adequate research.

	Yes	No
1. Read the essay question carefully		
Have you underlined or highlighted key words?	☐	☐
Have you looked up any word or phrase you do not understand?	☐	☐
Do you understand what the question is asking?	☐	☐
2. Plan the essay		
Have you constructed an outline plan?	☐	☐
Have you listed paragraph headings?	☐	☐
3. Carry out adequate research		
Have you regularly referred to the essay question?	☐	☐
Have you taken notes to support each paragraph heading?	☐	☐
Have you underlined/highlighted key words and ideas?	☐	☐

Remember, when carrying out research you should use a variety of resources.
The three listed below should be used for every essay.

Have you referred to resources used in class?	☐	☐
Have you used "Get Results"?	☐	☐
Have you referred to your own notes?	☐	☐
Have you used other resources, e.g., ICT?	☐	☐

please list ....

4.   When *writing the essay* for homework or classwork you should always include:

(a)   an introduction;

(b)   a main part;

(c)   a conclusion.

	Yes	No
5. The introduction		
Have you included a summary of the main points to be developed?	☐	☐
Have you included quotations?	☐	☐
Have you used Modern Studies terms?	☐	☐
Is the introduction brief?	☐	☐

Student Self Assessment Cont.

Modern Studies Higher Paper 1
Homework and Classwork

6. **The main part**

   Have you developed relevant points? ☐ ☐

   Have you explained difficult terminology? ☐ ☐

   Have you provided examples of people, places, events, statistics? ☐ ☐

   Have you included quotations, diagrams, sketches? ☐ ☐

   Have you offered reasons? ☐ ☐

   Have you offered opinions (not necessarily your own)

   supported by evidence? ☐ ☐

   Have you compared information/opinions, contrasted views,

   qualified statements? ☐ ☐

7. **Have you summarised the main points in your conclusion?** ☐ ☐

8. **Have you written in good, clear English?** ☐ ☐

9. **Have you used sufficient information to answer the question set?** ☐ ☐

10. **Is your information correct?** ☐ ☐

11. **Is your information relevant?** ☐ ☐

12. **Is your information wide enough in scope
    to answer the question set?** ☐ ☐

13. **Have you answered the question set?** ☐ ☐

Student Self Assessment

Modern Studies Higher Paper 2
Evaluating Questions

Please tick where appropriate

1. **When evaluating sources, did you**
    spend about 11 minutes on this part of the task read each source carefully making notes on:

    origin and reliability of each source ☐
    inaccuracies ☐
    selective use of facts ☐
    exaggeration ☐
    bias ☐
    conflicting lines of argument ☐
    contradictions ☐
    differing viewpoints ☐
    trends ☐
    important information, e.g. statistics ☐
    unusual information ☐

2. **When answering the evaluating questions, did you**

    read and understand each question ☐
    refer to your notes ☐
    use only the sources you were directed to ☐
    keep your answers brief ☐
    develop points rather than list them ☐
    leave out your own background knowledge ☐
    take about 9 minutes to write your answers ☐
    check over each answer ☐

Student Self Assessment

Modern Studies Higher Paper 2
The Decision-Making Task

Please tick where appropriate

1. **Before writing, did you**
    understand your role ☐
    consider the decision-making options available ☐
    evaluate the sources ☐
    make your decision ☐
    plan your final report ☐

2. **In your introduction, did you**
    state your role and remit ☐
    list the options ☐
    state your decision ☐

3. **In your report, have you included**
    use of your own background knowledge ☐
    reference to a wide range of given sources ☐
    well developed arguments covering:
        reasons for your decision ☐
        reasons why other options have been rejected ☐
        reasons against/problems/difficulties/
        criticisms arising from your decision ☐

4. **In your conclusion, did you**
    restate your decision ☐
    summarise briefly the main arguments ☐
    refer briefly to rejected options ☐
    commend your decision to others ☐

5. **When organising your time, did you**
    read the sources and decision-making task ☐
    complete and check over evaluating questions ☐
    plan, write and check over the decision-making task ☐
    complete a final check ☐